CHAMPIONSHIP COACHES

NICK SABAN

JOHN FREDRIC EVANS

Enslow Publishing
101 W. 23rd Street
Suite 240
New York, NY 10011
USA
enslow.com

Published in 2020 by Enslow Publishing, LLC
101 W. 23rd Street, Suite 240, New York, NY 10011

Library of Congress Cataloging-in-Publication Data

Names: Evans, John Fredric, author.
Title: Nick Saban / by John Fredric Evans.
Description: New York : Enslow Publishing, 2020. | Series: Championship coaches | Includes bibliographical references and index. | Audience: Grade 7-12.
Identifiers: LCCN 2017055234| ISBN 9780766098039 (library bound) | ISBN 9780766098046 (pbk.)
Subjects: LCSH: Saban, Nick—Juvenile literature. | Football coaches—United States—Biography—Juvenile literature. | University of Alabama—Football—Juvenile literature. | Alabama Crimson Tide (Football team)—Juvenile literature.
Classification: LCC GV939.S35 E83 2018 | DDC 796.332092 [B] —dc23
LC record available at https://lccn.loc.gov/2017055234

Printed in China

Photo Credits: Cover, pp. 1, 87 Christian Petersen/Getty Images; p. 5 Streeter Lecka/Getty Images; pp. 8, 13, 21, 46, 58, 75 © AP Images; p. 10 Scott Halleran/Getty Images; pp. 15, 80 Collegiate Images/Getty Images; p. 17 David Madison/Getty Images; p. 23 Jonathan Daniel/Getty Images; p. 25 Mike Powell/Getty Images; p. 30 Focus on Sport/Getty Images; p. 32 Rick Stewart/Getty Images; p. 34 Jed Jacobsohn/Getty Images; p. 36 Jeff Gross/Getty Images; p. 40 Mark Lyons/Getty Images; p. 50 Erik S. Lesser/Getty Images; p. 55 Jamie Squire/Getty Images; p. 61 Joe Robbins/Getty Images; p. 63 Eliot J. Schechter/Getty Images; p. 67 Andy Lyons/Getty Images; pp. 72, 83 Kevin C. Cox/Getty Images; p. 77 Orlando Sentinel/Tribune News Service/Getty Images; p. 91 Icon Sportswire/Getty Images.

CONTENTS

INTRODUCTION

It isn't every day that a football coach popularizes a philosophy for life, but that's just what Nick Saban has done with "The Process." The methodology he developed with Dr. Lionel Rosen is intended to streamline the pursuit of large, complex goals in a way that minimizes anxiety, confusion, and distraction. While he didn't invent process thinking, he has proven it works in the high-stakes, large-scale arena of college football.

Thanks to this widely imitated approach and a personality that makes him both infuriating and unstoppable, the two-time AP Coach of the Year stands on the threshold of becoming the greatest college football coach of all time. Only Bear Bryant has hoisted as many national championship trophies as Saban (six). It seems as though a Saban-coached team is always in the title game, or at least the favorite to get there, so the countdown is on.

Like his father, whose standards of excellence he could never reach, Saban is a hard man, and a hard man to like—unless he coaches your favorite football team. Many believe he is overpaid, at least in the sense that no mere football coach should earn several million dollars per year.

Nick Saban hoists the third of his six NCAA national championship trophies. One more and the coach breaks his tie with Bear Bryant for the all-time record.

Yet, in 2013, University of Alabama chancellor Dr. Robert Witt told *60 Minutes* that Saban was "the best financial investment this university has ever made … We have made an investment that's been returned many fold."[1] With Saban at the helm of its football team, the school found it easy to complete a fundraising campaign to upgrade aging facilities. In 2016, the SEC Network, a joint venture with ESPN, produced $39 million in revenue distribution for the University of Alabama alone, in no small part because people want to watch Nick Saban's team play football.

Beneath his often-harsh exterior, Saban is a sensitive man who has poured his heart into his passion— football—but is the first to take a fatherly role with a player who needs it. The man other coaches have called "the Devil" is a regular guy who eats two Little Debbie snack cakes every morning as he drinks coffee and checks the Weather Channel to see if his team will practice indoors or out. When practice begins, he's the little man in a straw golf hat, studiously taking notes. For lunch, it's always an iceberg lettuce salad topped with turkey slices. *This* is the mercenary, win-at-all-costs figure even Alabama fans often call "Our Dark Lord" on RollBamaRoll.com?

Perhaps that underlying humanity is why Saban has always had a knack for connecting with people of different races and income levels, from millionaires to ordinary folks. Whatever the reason, he has proven to be one of the greatest recruiters of all time. In Saban's decade at Alabama, the team has finished with the top recruiting class in the 247Sports Composite Team Rankings seven times.

You don't win at everything without being ultra competitive as a person, and Saban certainly is. Whether it's WaveRunner races, staff basketball games, golf, or tubing, he always wants to finish in first place. But for Saban, winning actually *isn't* everything. Doing it *right* is everything. He addressed the topic in his 2005 motivational book, *How Good Do You Want to Be?* "Win, lose—these are words we speak in college football. If you show up to compete with your very best preparation and effort, then you honor yourself and your team. Regardless of the outcome, you cannot truly lose."[2]

1

COULD HE EVER MAKE DAD PROUD?

The story of Nick Saban begins with his father, whom most people called "Big Nick." The son of a Croatian immigrant, Big Nick was born in the Appalachian foothills of West Virginia. He opened a service station situated in the midst of several small mining towns. This entrepreneurial venture was the only thing that spared him the backbreaking, perilous life of a coal miner.

> ***"Invest your time, don't spend it."*[1]**
> **—"Big Nick" Saban**

Operating a rural gas station did not provide a comfortable living, but it was enough to support a family. Barely. Big Nick married Mary Conaway, and they had two children in quick succession, Dianna in 1950 and Nick Jr. in 1951.

Saban went to high school in Monongah, West Virginia. The town is best known for 1907's deadly series of explosions in two of its coal mines.

The station was full service, and Big Nick put his son to work as soon as he was old enough to pump gas, wipe windshields, and wash cars. Saban often talks about how the cars he'd just washed would receive a careful examination from his father—if a single spot was missed, the boy would have to start over. "At the time, I could not understand his standard of excellence," said Saban. "But what I learned from my days at the gas station was to do a job right and not settle for anything less than the best. And that it takes hard work to do it the right way."[2]

AN EARLY START

Nick Jr. was recruiting from the age of ten, helping his father convince kids to join their Pop Warner football team, the Idamay Black

Diamonds. Big Nick and his partner named the team after the most-desired type of coal, anthracite. Football was a focal point of culture in their part of the country. In the first half of the twentieth century, the game was largely played by the strapping, rough-and-tumble sons of coal miners and steelworkers. They used the game to escape the same mines and mills Nick Sr. avoided by opening his own small business. "Football was hugely important to the towns and communities of that region: It united them,"[3] wrote Saban biographer Monte Burke in *Saban: The Making of a Coach.*

Under Big Nick, Black Diamond practices were long and extremely physical. "I worked harder in Pop Warner than I ever did in high school, college or the pros,"[4] said Nick's lifelong friend Kerry Marbury. His was one of many African American families living near Nick's grandparents, whom he visited often. Despite the general segregation of the times, the kids became friends at age six. "We're probably the first generation in our area that

Pop Warner Goes Way Back

In 1929, Joseph J. Tomlin founded what would become Pop Warner football in Philadelphia, with the hope that football would keep kids occupied and reduce the area's widespread vandalism. By 1933, the league had expanded from four to sixteen teams and Tomlin asked football legend Glenn "Pop" Warner to address the kids. When the evening came, the players were spellbound by him. It was immediately decided that the organization would be renamed in Warner's honor. Today, more than half a million youths participate in Pop Warner–sanctioned football programs every year.

could play together, and those relationships are still important to me,"[5] said Nick.

After practice, Big Nick made his players run up and down a steep hill. If the sun had already gone down he made them bring back a leaf from the trees on the ridgeline, to prove they made it to the top. The team won due to effort and intensity, not fancy plays, but they won a lot. In their third year of existence the Black Diamonds won the West Virginia State Championship without allowing a single point all season, part of a thirty-nine-game winning streak. In later years, the team would twice beat a Pop Warner team quarterbacked by a kid named Joe Montana—who would go on to become a superstar player for the San Francisco 49ers.

To this day, many kids' first exposure to organized football comes at the Pop Warner level.

Despite all their success, the players didn't get a lot of praise from their coach. It just wasn't in his nature. In fact, Big Nick was harder on his son than anyone. He expected the same perfection on the field that he did at the service station. Even when Nick Jr. threw a touchdown pass—and he threw a lot of them—Big Nick would find something to improve on, whether it was a strategic flaw like a missed read or a loose spiral. As his son remembers it, "All our mistakes were opportunities to get better. 'It's not just about the results,' [Big Nick] would tell us. 'It's about perfect execution.'"[6]

Big Nick wasn't a man you wanted mad at you. "He was old school in every sense of the term," Saban said of his father. "He had an air about him that commanded respect—even a little bit of fear. I'm not talking about being mean, just tough. Toughness was important to him. And that meant having the work ethic to get things right."[7]

> ***"It was just tough love. We knew [Big Nick] cared for us."[8]***
> **—Kerry Marbury**

It was also important to Big Nick that his son excelled in school. Nick was too shy to sing in his eighth grade music class, which resulted in a D on his report card. Seeing this, his father made him quit all sports and, with help from miner friends, took him to the darkest depths of the local coal mine. "When we reached the bottom, he turned to me, his face glowing red in the deep black. 'Is this what you want? You want to work down here the rest of your life?'"[9] Message received. Saban sang in music class and graduated high school as a member of the National Honor Society.

LOVE AND FRIENDSHIP

From Pop Warner through high school, Nick played football with his friend Kerry Marbury, who had grown into a gifted running back. The chemistry they developed on the field carried over to high school, where the duo led Monongah High to a state championship. Despite his short stature—five feet six inches (170 centimeters) at most—Nick was an exceptional three-sport athlete. He earned all-state honors in football, basketball, and baseball.

Big Nick occasionally took his son to West Virginia University practices or games, and they bonded over in-depth discussions of gridiron strategy. If Kerry was at their house, he'd often leave when the pair trooped into the TV room to watch 8mm game film. "The two of them would sit there and watch for hours, and love it,"[10] Nick Sr. said. The knowledge and preparation gained in this ritual gave Nick a leg up on his competition. It was an edge he later sought as a coach.

Mama Saban

Nick's mother, Mary, counterbalanced her husband's strict parenting style. She was warm-hearted and had a serene, approachable demeanor. With a father who seemed impossible to please, Nick needed her to instill him with confidence. "You need somebody to pat you on the back, somebody to rub your neck a little bit and help you keep your chin up," Saban said. "And my mom always did that."[11]

During his senior year of high school, Nick met a girl. When he saw Terry Constable at a football game, he knew he had to talk to her. This wasn't their first meeting; in eighth grade they'd clicked at a science camp and she invited him to go bird-watching … at five a.m. Not only was that way too early for a date, in Nick's mind, but he had a softball game at eight, and he wasn't about to miss that.

Nick's wife, Terry, seen here in 2009, is his closest confidante and advisor in all his career decisions.

Nick had regretted this decision, but fortunately it all worked out. Terry gave him a second chance, and the pair would share a lifelong love. Today, after pregame warmups, Terry is always there waiting with a kiss when Nick trots back to the locker room. At the end of every game she is the first person he seeks out for a hug and another kiss.

"Going back forty years to when we first met at that summer science camp, my admiration for and belief in Terry has only grown stronger," said Saban. "She has made many sacrifices for our family, and her strength has allowed me to pursue coaching. Don't think for a minute that I wouldn't give it all up for her. I would. Thing is, she wouldn't ask me to."[12]

2

MASTERING THE MENTAL GAME

Nick was too small and slow to secure an athletic scholarship to West Virginia, so he went to Kent State University in Ohio. There, he switched to safety and applied his understanding of offense to the other side of the ball. On defense, his smarts and toughness more than compensated for his athletic shortcomings. His best friend in college was teammate Phil Witherspoon, who was African American. "Nick was really blind to color, and this was during a time of some real racial unrest in the country," said Saban's roommate, Steve Broderick. "I always noticed that there seemed to be no difference for him."[1]

Future NFL Hall of Famer Jack Lambert, legendary for his hard-nosed, big-hitting play, was the team's starting middle linebacker in 1972. Quarterback Greg Kokal delivered the ultimate compliment when he said that "Lambert had better skills, but Nick was tougher."[2]

After more than two years in a long-distance relationship, Nick married Terry during his junior year. She then enrolled at Kent State and joined him in student housing. These were lean times with very little money, as the couple lived on peanut butter and jelly sandwiches, tomato soup, and grilled cheese. At night Nick loaded trucks, and Terry worked in the school registrar's office. "We didn't have much, but we had each other, and we were true partners,"[3] said Saban.

Nick's Kent State University teammate Jack Lambert would go on to win four Super Bowls with the Pittsburgh Steelers.

FINDING A MENTOR

> ***"Many times it is not the plan that failed, but rather the implementation of it."***[4]
>
> **—Nick Saban**

After the infamous Kent State shootings, where the Ohio National Guard opened fire on college students protesting the Vietnam War, the university's football coach quit and young Don James was hired to take over. James was the kind of leader Saban aspired to become. "Coach

Brush with Death

On May 4, 1970, Kent State student Nick Saban left class near a large rally protesting the US invasion of Cambodia. He convinced his friend to get lunch instead of watching the protest. Inexperienced members of the Ohio National Guard confronted the crowd, panicked, and opened fire. When the smoke cleared, four students were dead and nine were wounded. A few minutes later, Saban wandered through the scene in shock. Among the dead was Allison Krause, an honors student with whom Saban shared an English class. He later told *USAToday* "there's not a May 4th that goes by that I don't think about it."[5]

James was extremely organized and had a good system and a good staff in place," said Saban. "He did everything with a certain level of class that I admired, and he treated you in a way that made you feel special."[6]

After Saban got his degree, he accepted a job as a graduate assistant on James's coaching staff. This experience certainly prepared him for the future. Saban did recruiting, evaluated players, and took film to be developed at Pittsburgh Steelers' headquarters, where he got to know defensive line coach George Perles. "We'd have a beer sometimes after practice and he'd just pick my brain about football," said Perles. "I liked him."[7]

When Saban left home, he began a weekly tradition of calling his father after the game on Saturday. He was excited to be working under a mentor like Don James, and it had given him some clarity on his future plans. Saban remembers the last conversation he had with Big Nick, minutes after his first win as an assistant coach. "I said 'Dad, this is what I want to do. I know this is what I want to do.' That was the last conversation I had. I told him what I wanted to do, and that was to be a coach."[8]

Despite his unsentimental demeanor, Big Nick remained committed to coaching until the end of his life. A doctor told him that he should quit because of the strain it put on his bad heart. He refused. He kept supporting young football players, building the character of hundreds of kids over the years. If someone needed shoes but couldn't afford them, he would provide them. At forty-six years old, Big Nick suffered a fatal heart attack during a jog home. Inscribed on his tombstone is the epitaph "No man stands as tall as when he stoops to help a child." The Black Diamonds' old field is now named after Nick Saban Sr.

Don James, seen here in 1982, was a key mentor for Saban.

After his father's sudden death, Saban felt obligated to move home and run the service station. His mother and Coach James convinced him not to abandon his dreams. By then Kerry Marbury was playing in the Canadian Football League. When his request to attend Big Nick's funeral was refused, he went anyway and was cut from the team. He never regretted it.

In 1973, Saban witnessed Don James's turnaround of a struggling team, which finished 9–2. Nick admired the fact that his boss made sure every member of the organization knew exactly what was expected of them. James was also a stickler for details and seemed to have a system for everything. Saban would employ many of James's methods in his own coaching career.

After James went to Washington, where he would ultimately win a national championship with the Huskies, Saban stayed at Kent State until the end of the 1976 season. With James's recommendation, Saban was hired at Syracuse to coach linebackers and defensive ends. He was an intense and exacting leader, even then. "Saban wasn't out there to make friends," said Dennis Hartman, a fullback on the team. "He was feisty, and pretty tough on his players."[9]

Saban's job security was shaky, the winters were harsh in upstate New York, and Terry was homesick, so after the 1977 season he accepted an offer to be the assistant coach at West Virginia University. Saban only learned later that Terry had secretly worked behind the scenes to orchestrate their return home. It would not be the last time that his wife played a key role in his career moves.

> ***"In my three decades of coaching, I've learned that process is much more important than result."***[10]
>
> **—Nick Saban**

As a kid, Saban had dreamed of playing for his home-state school. The job seemed like a perfect fit, as the campus was just 20 miles (32 kilometers) from home. He proved a more-than-able recruiter who made African American athletes feel comfortable with the idea of playing at a mostly white school. He was also adept at mapping out a recruit's whole career for him, anticipating potential objections and addressing them. These skills would serve him well in the years to come.

Unfortunately, the West Virginia Mountaineers struggled and the university fired its head coach at the end of the 1979 season. Ohio State offered Saban a job as secondary coach and he accepted, joining two friends and former colleagues who'd lobbied hard for him. The Buckeyes were a perennial powerhouse in college football, so this was a huge step forward for Saban. It also made recruiting much easier for him, given the impressive reputation of the program.

CHANGE IS THE ONLY CONSTANT

Problems arose, however, when Saban clashed with head coach Earl Bruce over how to defend the pass-first offenses becoming popular at that time. Though they were the wave of the future, not only in college but also in the NFL, old-fashioned coaches didn't want to reevaluate the kinds of players they used in the secondary. Saban was proven right as even unranked opponents shredded the Buckeyes through the air in 1981. As stopping the pass was Saban's responsibility, he received the blame for the defense's struggles. What's more, he was forced to start three sophomores and one freshman. Under his tutelage, they improved greatly in the course of the year. When Saban was allowed to craft a game plan to stop Michigan star

Anthony Carter, his charges neutralized the gifted wide receiver and Ohio State snared three interceptions in a 14–9 upset win.

It was too little, too late, however, and the defensive coaching staff—including Saban—was fired after the season. It was the first and only time he was relieved of his duties as a coach. In Dennis Fryzel's exit interview, the defensive coordinator said, "I'll take the hit for the defense, but the best football coach on this whole staff is Nick Saban. He's the best recruiter. I'll take the shot, but don't fire Nick."[11]

Though Fryzel would be a lifelong friend, his pleas fell on deaf ears. Saban was let go. Of the firing, he said: "I questioned not only my career choice, but my abilities as well. I had failed. I was devastated and humiliated."[12] Saban's players showed up at his house with a plaque that read, "Thanks for the confidence this season and we'll miss you as a coach and a friend."[13]

Another friend, Gary Tranquill, became the head coach at Navy in 1982 and offered Saban a job. This was a promotion, in the sense

Airing It Out

In the old days, football was all about the running game. Offenses seldom threw the ball, and defenses focused on stopping the run. Forward-thinking coaches began to realize that big, strong defenders lacked the ability to keep up with fleet-footed receivers. They took advantage of this by passing against tight and heavy formations. What's more, a long pass completion picks up many more yards than most runs. Smaller colleges whose players lacked the size to win toe-to-toe in the trenches began to surpass the pedigreed programs with strategic quickness. More and more teams, first in college and then in the pros, found success through the air against burly defenders.

that Saban would run the whole defense. Saban surprised the team by walking in with a suit on and a briefcase in hand, presenting the kind of corporate polish he would later bring into home visits with the families of recruits.

Saban greets his friend Bill Belichick before the Dolphins beat the Patriots 28–26 in January 2006.

Though he left after just one season at Navy, Saban made an important connection in his tour with the Midshipmen. He befriended scout and assistant coach Steve Belichick, whose son Bill was on the staff of the New York Giants at the time. In the summer, Bill came home and spent many evenings on his father's front porch, talking football with Saban. The pair spent hours dissecting every aspect of the game they loved. "Nick is a great defensive coach, but he understands everything about offensive football and how to attack and defend the offensive schemes used on the other side of the ball,"[14] said Bill Belichick, who would later win six Super Bowls as head coach of the New England Patriots.

This relationship would prove mutually beneficial a few years down the road.

3

MAKE A DIFFERENCE AND MOVE ON

The next stop for Saban was Michigan State, where George Perles was now the head coach. Perles added his old friend to the staff in 1983. Not only was Saban a good coach, he was a fun guy to be around. Though they were paddleball partners and bar buddies, Perles knew that Saban's social side was about networking as much as companionship. Saban had his sights set on a head-coaching job, and he wouldn't get that opportunity without making the necessary connections. "He worked hard, was in early, and stayed late," said Perles. "He was a teacher and he was interested in moving up. He was good at what he did, and the kids who played for him respected him and liked him. He was everything you wanted in a coach."[1]

As Michigan State's head coach, Nick looks on as Purdue beats the Spartans in 1997. Win or lose, he always wants his team to think about what's next.

Saban stayed with the Spartans for five years, gradually developing into a viable head-coaching candidate. Though Saban had been hired to coach the secondary, after the first year he was entrusted with designing the defensive game plan. His pursuit of perfection would have made Big Nick proud. Saban focused on fundamentals and held players accountable for the slightest miscue seen on game film. As a recruiter, he brought a number of star prospects into the fold. His approach was to offer players a challenge, not promises of playing time on the field. The more competitive the player, the more appealing this was.

> ***"For the first time, I thought to myself that I could be a head coach."[2]***
>
> **—Nick Saban**

In 1986, Nick and Terry adopted a child, Nicholas. A few years later, they completed the "matched set" with a girl, Kristen. "I worked just as hard at my job as I did being a father and maintained the same standard of excellence in both," said Saban. "I still want to be a great dad. It is a job I have never stopped trying to get better at."[3]

It was at MSU that Saban learned the importance of off-season conditioning. The strength and conditioning coaches he later hired were all disciples of Carl "Buck" Nystrom, who ran a grueling fitness program under Perles. Something else that Saban picked up from Perles was his "twenty-four-hour rule." After a win or a loss—regardless of its significance—the players, coaches, and staff had one day to celebrate or second-guess and then it was time to move on. Saban adopted this with his own teams and came to live by it.

Fresh in the Fourth

Former Michigan State assistant coach Carl "Buck" Nystrom is the originator of the mentally and physically demanding "Fourth Quarter" conditioning program, which puts players through a grueling series of drills and workouts in the winter. Currently run by Alabama strength and conditioning coach Scott Cochran, the program takes its name from the concept that players should have the same energy and intensity in the game's final quarter as its first. Late in games, "Fourth Quarter" alums often hold up four fingers, which represent discipline, effort, toughness, and commitment.

SUCCESS ISN'T ENOUGH

By 1987, the Michigan State defense was ranked No. 2 in the country. Saban's players helped notch a huge win when, in week five, the Spartans intercepted seven UMich passes on their way to a 17–11 win. Then Saban earned a measure of revenge against the coach who had fired him when his defense shut down Ohio State's passing game in Columbus, using the lighter, swifter kind of safeties Earl Bruce wouldn't let Saban have when he oversaw the Buckeyes' secondary. The 13–7 defeat began a three-game losing streak that cost Bruce his own job.

Michigan State finished 8–2–1 and won the Big Ten, which earned them a date with USC in the Rose Bowl. Once again Saban's stoppers got the job done, pressuring talented USC quarterback Rodney Peete relentlessly and forcing four turnovers. The final score was 20–17, Spartans.

In the 1988 Rose Bowl, Saban's disciplined defense held USC in check and Michigan State won 20–17.

In classic Saban fashion, he stuck out like a sore thumb in the jubilant locker room. A local reporter asked him what was wrong and he responded, "Did you see what they did to my defense?"[4] Saban was hung up on the fact that Peete had led a few long drives. He's admitted that he's just not wired to accept success. "I enjoy success, but it's only because I'm happy for the players and assistants and the thousands of fans and supporters who are pleased with what we accomplished," said Saban. "My father always taught me that you shouldn't be satisfied with success—someone is always waiting to challenge that success in the next game."[5]

By this point Saban was also feeling restless in his supporting role. But the head-coaching jobs he hoped for didn't quite materialize, so he found another way to move up in the world. Recommendations from football minds such as Bill Belichick prompted Houston Oilers coach Jerry Glanville to take a chance on the thirty-six-year-old despite his lack of NFL experience. "It was a difficult adjustment for me, but I had to put my ego aside and learn and grow with the new experience,"[6] said Saban.

Glanville was a playful eccentric who shot from the hip, the opposite of the buttoned-up, ever-serious Saban. While he wouldn't be borrowing many specifics of Glanville's unorthodox coaching style, Saban adopted his "challenge every pass" philosophy.

The defensive backs Saban coached were not only well-paid professional athletes, they were also a nasty group whose hard-hitting style of play earned their stadium the nickname "the House of Pain."

These grizzled vets were intimidating both on the field and off. Saban and his secondary clashed because he rode Pro Bowlers as hard as rookies. Tensions boiled over in a meeting one day and Saban got into a physical confrontation with safety Keith Bostic. Eventually, though, the players bought into Saban's scheme and it paid dividends. In the playoffs, the Oilers short-circuited Cleveland's passing game in a 24–23 win. The next week they limited Buffalo's explosive aerial attack, but the offense let them down in a 17–10 road loss.

WHOLLY TOLEDO?

By the midpoint of the following season, Saban was again seeking his first head-coaching gig. He got the blessing of his boss, and Glanville even practiced interview questions with Saban to get him prepared. He aced an interview at the University of Toledo and landed the job. Fulfilling his obligations in Houston, Saban guided his secondary to a strong performance against Pittsburgh in the postseason. But despite limiting the Steelers to a mere 112 passing yards, the Oilers were again undone by their offense and lost in overtime, 26–23.

At Toledo, Saban entered a fairly good situation. It wasn't a high-profile school in a major conference, but the Rockets were talented enough to be considered a preseason favorite. After being challenged or ignored by veterans on the Oilers, Saban wasn't going to stand for any of that here. In his first meeting with the players, he told juniors and seniors their experience didn't guarantee their jobs and starting roles were open to competition. Toledo's best defensive player, Dan Williams, questioned him before the group and, without hesitation, Saban told him he was off the team. Williams was so talented he'd later be taken in the first round of the NFL Draft, so the locker room saw there'd be no free passes given, no matter how impressive the athlete was.

A few players quit, and Williams was allowed to return after accepting disciplinary action, but the players who trusted Saban's leadership quickly saw the benefits of his system. The Rockets finished the 1990 season 9–2 and were conference cochampions. Despite the success, Saban was later critical of his own coaching in Toledo. He admitted to coaching defensively, both literally and figuratively, because he worried what others would think if his plays failed. "I was fearful of criticism and failure," he said. "I soon learned that you can never please everybody, and you can't worry about what others think—you have to do what you believe to be right in the situation."[7]

It looked like the beginning of a prosperous era for the program, but then Saban got a call from Bill Belichick. The coach was coming off the 1991 Super Bowl, where his brilliant game plan limited a top-flight offense to nineteen points in the Giants' one-point victory over the Buffalo Bills. He'd just been hired by the Cleveland Browns, his first NFL head-coaching job, and he wanted Saban to be his defensive coordinator.

BUILDING A DEFENSE

As with most of his career moves, Saban agonized over the decision. He knew he was leaving Toledo in the lurch, and his family was happy there. In Saban's explanatory press conference, he was visibly emotional. "I haven't cried for eighteen years—since my dad died—but I cried all afternoon. It was something I just couldn't pass up … It's probably not fair to the University of Toledo. It's a little bit of a selfish decision. But I have a responsibility to my family."[8]

The reasons to leave were compelling. Saban and Belichick saw eye-to-eye on many things and had wanted to build a team together since their porch chats in Annapolis. And if Saban took the job, his pay would more than double.

In Cleveland, Belichick gave Saban significant control over personnel and scheme. He'd need it to rebuild a defense that allowed more points in 1990 than any defense would in the entire decade. Never in his career was Belichick more demanding than with the Browns, and even Saban's legendary work ethic was tested to the breaking point in the course of countless eighteen-hour days. But his tireless labors paid off as the defense improved from dreadful to middle of the pack in one season. In his

Birds of a Feather

While Bill Belichick came from a more prosperous upbringing, he, like Saban, was obsessed with football from a young age. Both had fathers who coached and were their first mentors in the sport. Belichick made his name as a detail-oriented defensive assistant and coordinator who expected his players to do their jobs with the same absolute dedication he did, too. Belichick's sternly professional demeanor has been subject to the same criticism as Saban's. And both coaches consider preparation the most important part of the game. Saban has won five national championships and Belichick five Super Bowls.

second year, the defense went thirteen quarters without allowing a touchdown and finished tenth best in the NFL.

> ***"I don't believe in tired."*** [9]
>
> **—Nick Saban**

Linebacker Dont'a Hightower has played for both Saban, in college, and Belichick, in the NFL. "Nick and Bill were obviously close friends when they coached together in Cleveland," said Hightower. "It doesn't surprise me how much success they have when you look at how much they live, breathe and die football. They're literally the exact same." [10]

The year 1993 was a difficult one for the Browns. Belichick cut loose popular veterans, eroding the trust of the players left behind. Saban thought this caused the team to lose focus, which he believed was the biggest mental downfall a team can suffer. "Focus is an ability to zero in on what's important and being able to avoid distractions to complete the task," he wrote in his 2005 book, *How Good Do You Want to Be?* [11]

When he coached the Cleveland Browns, Bill Belichick seized the opportunity to hire Saban as his defensive coordinator.

If 1993 was a step back, the 1994 campaign was two steps forward and would catapult Saban to the next level in his career.

4

FLIRTATIONS AND FORMIDABLE TEAMS

By the 1994 season, the Browns veterans had mixed feelings about Saban, whose nickname was "Grumpy." One player said of Saban, "He was kind of a little tyrant walking around out there."[1] Saban admitted later that he needed to change. "We all make mistakes in our professional and personal lives, so you just have to accept that you are not perfect," he wrote in his book. "It's how you react to mistakes that can move you toward, or away from, success. Early on in my career, I thought ranting and raving about a dropped

years without a winning season. Knowing the head coach position was a promotion for Saban, Belichick supported his candidacy. Saban wowed his interviewers with his detailed plan to turn the program around and his confidence that he'd do just that. Saban instituted mandatory study halls and training meals to support his players' grades and nutrition. He established the goal of each player graduating with the tools to be successful in life, whether or not football was involved. "Keep in mind that the majority of our players will never earn a dollar playing football,"[5] he said.

"Peer intervention programs" put disciplinary power in the hands of players selected by their peers. This gave team leaders a stake in the creation and enforcement of the rules governing their behavior, in and outside of team activities. Saban's new staff included the Spartans' highly successful future head coach, Mark Dantonio, and strength and conditioning coach Ken Mannie. At every stop Saban would have someone like Mannie, an "alpha dog" personality who put players through the arduous "Fourth Quarter" program. "We try to get to a point where there's nothing they will face in a game,

Led by coach Tom Osborne, the Nebraska Cornhuskers built a winning program in the 1990s.

from a physical and effort and discipline and toughness standpoint, that they haven't faced before,"[6] said Mannie.

As always, Saban put his heart and soul into his job for as long as he was there. Terry likes to tell the story that over that first summer at Michigan State, Saban met a friend at an East Lansing bar and, as usual, became deeply engrossed in a football conversation. Apparently an armed robber confronted the cashier, not twenty feet (6.1 m) away. Saban never even noticed.

GROWING PAINS

The Michigan State Spartans opened the 1995 season by hosting the defending national champions, the Nebraska Cornhuskers. The visitors won 50–10, and Nebraska head coach Tom Osborne consoled Saban afterward by saying, "You're not as bad as you think."[7] That would become evident in the course of the year, as Nebraska pulverized every opponent they faced en route to their second-straight championship. "I learned a lesson that day," said Saban. "As long as you do this,

A Standard Set

Under coach Tom Osborne, the Nebraska Cornhuskers were a dominant force in the 1990s. The team won a staggering 95 percent of its games in a five-year span and claimed back-to-back national championships in 1994 and 1995, with a share of a third in 1997. Built on defense and a strong running game, the Huskers' bruising brand of football physically overwhelmed the opposition. Perhaps the greatest college team ever, the 1995 team outscored opponents by an average of 53–14, outgained them by 264 yards per game, and never trailed after the second quarter. Saban says Osborne's teams provided the blueprint he follows.

it's always about your next play. It's always about the next game."[8]

In fact, Saban's first season was seen as a success. Despite being pegged as a team likely to underperform, Michigan State University went 6–5–1, the school's first winning record in five years. Terry flourished in the role of coach's wife, her grace and warmth compensating for Saban's rough edges. She also proved just as detail-oriented as her husband, handling his off-field affairs and even interviewing prospective coaches.

Though Saban can struggle with his short game, he is a serious golfer whose best attribute is his focus.

Saban didn't tone down his overbearing style of leadership, but as Burnett predicted it was better received by college kids. Still, even then he wasn't just a strict taskmaster. Quarterback Tony Banks credits Saban with giving him the confidence to make his NFL aspirations a reality. (Banks was a second-round pick.) Linebacker Ike Reese is grateful that Saban held him accountable for his actions at a time in his life when he was troubled and immature. The tough love got Reese on the path to playing in the NFL for eight years.

Saban wasn't especially popular among assistant coaches, administrators, and boosters. He became known for a scornful look coaches dubbed "the bug zapper." But he could still turn on the charm for the parents of potential recruits, who generally loved him. He found out so much about the players and their families that talking to him was like talking to a friend. He also emphasized that his role was as much to prepare his players for life as for football games. "I tell them this is a forty-year decision, not a four-year one."[9]

Saban's second year was not a big step forward in terms of overall record, however, and as usual there were flirtations with other jobs, which concerned his employers. The New York Giants offered him a head coaching position, but he declined when they wouldn't assure him of enough decision-making power. Michigan State reacted to this by sweetening his contract substantially.

By now Saban was a local celebrity. He was invited to play a round of golf with Tiger Woods, then a megastar, at a PGA Pro-Am golf tournament during the Buick Open in Flint, Michigan. Saban was no more than an average golfer and he had certainly never played in front of fifteen thousand

The Brilliant Vagabond

The greatest coaches tend to be associated with one team. Casey Stengel and the Yankees. John Wooden and UCLA. Bear Bryant and Alabama. But some seem to relish taking over a program in tatters, leading it back to respectability, and moving on. One such turnaround artist is Larry Brown, the only coach in NBA history to guide eight different teams to the playoffs. Brown is the only coach to win both NBA and NCAA championships. Like Saban, he prefers college. "College kids want to be coached," said Brown. "They might resist it a little bit early on, but the more you give, the more you get back."[10]

fans. On one errant stroke, he plunked a spectator in the gallery. Afterward, Woods said that "Nick seemed a little nervous."[11] As always, Saban assessed his performance and reached conclusions. "My lack of focus came from a lack of experience in that situation,"[12] he said. Meanwhile, he took note of Woods's ability to approach every shot the same way—as if it were the eighteenth hole at the Masters—and sustain that sharp focus again and again.

> *"Michigan State is a place that's very dear to my heart."*[13]
>
> **—Nick Saban**

The Spartans' 1997 campaign began with great promise: a five-game winning streak that included a 23–7 victory at Notre Dame. Then they lost four in a row. A key factor in the skid was their kicking game. That year, and throughout Saban's career, missed field goals and blocked tries bedeviled his team. If a Saban team loses a game, such miscues are usually involved. But he did not get down on himself or the team and took a measured tone in his remarks after the fourth straight defeat. The team finished on a high note, winning its last two games to end the year 7–4. However, a loss in the Aloha Bowl dropped Saban's mark in bowl games to 0–3.

At this point, some commentators in the press called Saban overrated and it seemed his career might have been at a crossroads. He later acknowledged that he was much too conservative on offense in his first few years at MSU and lost games because of it. He would begin to open it up, but that was by no means the most important step in his evolution. That distinction goes to his association with Dr. Lionel Rosen.

5

PROCESS DRIVEN

The 1998 Michigan State Spartans were at an underwhelming 4–4 record, with four games to play, when Saban met one of his colleagues at the university, psychiatry professor Lionel "Lonny" Rosen. Saban had a keen interest in psychology so he was receptive to Rosen's views, which seemed to amplify his father's belief that perfect execution was the goal, not just a win or some other desired result. The unlikely duo also agreed that confusion and anxiety have only negative effects on performance and that football can be mentally and emotionally overwhelming. The pair broke down the many elements of a successful football season—games, practices, meetings—into smaller, more manageable goals. They got as granular as a single football play, training players to concentrate entirely on those seven seconds or so, rest, and then do it all again.

Quarterback Bill Burke celebrates the Spartans' 1998 upset of the Ohio State Buckeyes in Columbus. The win convinced Saban that Dr. Lonny Rosen's "process" made great things possible.

DEVELOPING "THE PROCESS"

The team's next game was on the road against Ohio State, that perennial powerhouse in the Big Ten and, at the time, the top team in the country. The Buckeyes were 28-point favorites and posting an average victory margin of 38–9. Leading up to the game, Saban saw that his team felt outmatched and doomed to be humiliated. Fortunately, he'd just met Rosen and had an epiphany that would change his coaching style forever. Starting in practice that week, each Spartan would focus on his individual responsibility, play by play, and entrust the big picture to Saban and his coaching staff. And, in his own way, Saban, too, would focus on one detail at a time. Everyone involved felt their stress and anxiety drain to a manageable level.

Even when Ohio State stormed to a 17–3 lead in the first quarter, then got a pick six early in the second half to lead 24–9, no one seemed to panic on the Michigan State side. They didn't look at the scoreboard or the game clock. Instead, they calmly and methodically scored 19 unanswered points to win 28–24, completing a colossal upset. Saban's friend and fellow former Ohio State assistant Dennis Fryzel was on the sidelines with him and, when the clock hit double zeroes, he planted a kiss right on Saban's lips.

The win was an instant, total validation of Rosen's philosophy, and he was Saban's most trusted advisor from that point on. Though Rosen would remain at MSU, he continued to work with Saban and counsel his players. But adopting "The Process" did not mean Michigan State went undefeated the rest of the way. They split their last four games to finish the year 6–6 and failed to qualify for a bowl game for the only time in Saban's tenure.

In 1999, the Spartans opened the year 5–0 and earned a No. 11 national ranking. Entering a grudge match with intrastate rival

One Step at a Time

What's known as "process thinking" originated in the 1960s, when psychiatrist Aaron Beck developed a therapy based on the idea that building good mental habits is done step by step. As employed in sports, this process has two key principles: to achieve the desired outcome one must focus only on the present, and even the most seemingly trivial action may affect that outcome. In other words: wins and losses must be forgotten, the task at hand demands full attention, and it's important to get the little things right. Other coaches have adopted Saban's version of "The Process."

Michigan, also undefeated and ranked No. 3, the Spartans were ready. The Wolverines were playing both Tom Brady (yes, that Tom Brady) and Drew Henson at quarterback, and the MSU defense harassed Henson particularly. Future NFL star Plaxico Burress notched 255 receiving yards in a thrilling 34–31 win for the Spartans. They beat Ohio State again and, with a 9–2 record, expected to play in one of the marquee bowl games. Instead, UMich got their bid, despite finishing with the same record and losing their head-to-head matchup.

Saban's perception that Michigan State would always be snubbed contributed to his decision to leave for Louisiana State University. Money was also a factor, as Saban's new agent Jimmy Sexton assured him he'd be more appreciated—and better compensated—in Baton Rouge. He also liked what his suitors had to offer. "At first I wasn't even interested, but the more I researched and saw the commitment of the LSU administrators, the more serious my interest in the challenge grew,"[2] Saban revealed in his book.

> ***"The thing that amazes me about him is that he doesn't let up."***[1]
>
> **—Bobby Bowden**

So he signed a five-year contract that made him the third-highest-paid coach in college football. The other two, Bobby Bowden and Steve Spurrier, had won national championships. Bowden had two.

The Michigan State administration, team, and fans felt betrayed, and it didn't make anyone feel better that Saban wasn't sure he'd done the right thing. The folks at LSU weren't absolutely certain he'd accept their offer until he said so publicly. "To this day I believe that had the Michigan State president called Nick at any time up until the moment he stepped up to the press conference, he could have Nick back,"[3] declared LSU trustee Charlie Weems.

EYE OF THE TIGER

The team Nick inherited was nothing special. The Tigers had managed to win more games than they lost in just three of the last eleven seasons. The team had the lowest graduation rate in the SEC. A number of players had been arrested or caught talking to agents, an NCAA violation. From a recruiting perspective, LSU lost some of Louisiana's best prep talent to other schools. One of the first things Saban did was tour the state's high schools, getting to know their coaches and making them feel important. Meanwhile, he scouted their players.

When recruiting in-state stars, Saban often told recruits things like, "You can go to one of those other schools in those other states, or you can come play for me and play for LSU and be part of a tradition in the state you love, where your pride is, and where you'll probably return."[4]

Giving a little boost to Saban's recruiting efforts was the fact that Terry mastered "bid whist," a bridge-like card game popular in the African American community. Among the families of many potential recruits, it made socializing easy and fun. She also ensured that Saban knew enough about household furnishings and decorating to discuss them knowledgeably with players' mothers.

The team went 7–4 in Saban's first season and earned a Peach Bowl bid, where they'd face Georgia Tech. Saban was keenly aware of his winless record in bowl games as a head coach. Going against his natural inclination but knowing he needed to change something, Saban gave the team more time off to rest, then focused on fundamentals for awhile before beginning to practice the game plan. The Tigers won 28–14, completing their rapid turnaround.

Fresh off this success, Saban had more to peddle in his recruiting visits and came back with a bumper crop of incoming freshmen. He landed nine of the top ten recruits in Louisiana. The class included future NFL players Michael Clayton (receiver), Joseph Addai (tailback), and Andrew Whitworth (tackle). LSU had seventeen starters returning, too. It added up to a No. 10 ranking in one preseason poll.

In the final game of the year, the Tigers were 7–3 and playing Auburn for the SEC West title. Stout defense and a solid running game powered them to a 27–14 triumph. Saban had led LSU to its first SEC Championship game, but the

A Dark Day

In the wake of the terrorist attacks of Tuesday, September 11, 2001, the SEC did not initially cancel the weekend's games. Saban continued work on his game plan for the next opponent and didn't broach the subject with his players in the course of the week. He later told a newspaper that he had his "head buried in the sand." When the NFL canceled the week's slate, the SEC postponed its games and Saban saw that his team was reeling. He offered players and staff words of comfort and later acknowledged there is such a thing as being *too* focused.

competition would be fierce. The Tennessee Volunteers were 10–1 and ranked No. 2 in the nation. They'd beaten LSU in the third game of the season and were certainly favored to do so again. Most pundits expected Tennessee to dispatch LSU and play in the Rose Bowl. Saban got more "bulletin board material" when he noticed that there were many boxes of rose petals on hand at the game, ready to fill the air when the Vols punched their ticket to the Rose Bowl.

> ***"Motivation itself generally lasts about two plays—it's highly overrated."***[5]
>
> **—Lionel Rosen**

While Saban uses every available method to conjure forth his players' best effort, he would agree with Rosen that getting a team "fired up" has little sustained effect on performance. "Motivation itself generally lasts about two plays—it's highly overrated," Rosen told the *Lansing State Journal* in 2003. "Give me a team that has a business-like attitude, a team that can deal with adversity when it comes."[6]

Saban emphasizes preparation, not inspiration. "Let me let you in on a little secret about football coaches," he wrote. "Very few of us have the skill, experience and education necessary to motivate a group of eighty men merely with a pregame speech."[7] Saban considers a pregame (or halftime) speech a time for reminders, though he occasionally plays to the emotion of the game. He spends the whole season trying to get his message through to the team and all week hammering home any game-specific points.

Saban helped linebacker Bradie James cope with personal tragedy during his time at LSU. James came to see football as a form of therapy.

It didn't look like preparation and motivation would be enough, at first. Tennessee led by 7 at the half, and Saban felt it necessary to replace his starting quarterback, who was getting mauled, with freshman Matt Mauck. The move paid off as the mobile passer led four second-half scoring drives and the Tigers pulled off a 31–20 upset. They went on to beat Illinois in the Sugar Bowl.

FATHER FIGURE

During this time Saban formed a special bond with nineteen-year-old linebacker Bradie James, whose father passed away a week before the Sugar Bowl. "It was devastating," said Saban. "For the rest of that year, I was as much a father as a coach to Bradie."[8] Saban choked up when sharing his feelings for his own father, who died young. "He said he wished his father was around to see his success,"[9] said James. On the day James's father was buried, both cried.

Shockingly, James's mother died three months later. Saban had no answers for him, but he could listen. In 2002, Saban often drove James to practice, giving fatherly advice along the way, and they shared emotional sessions with Dr. Rosen. They agreed that when coping with grief, finding one's passion in life and pursuing it was the best way to move on. James chose football. "It really became my outlet,"[10] he said, and he ultimately played ten seasons in the NFL.

After the 2001 season Saban was linked to vacancies in the NFL's head-coaching ranks, as well as to Notre Dame. But Saban was content with a salary bump and a new provision that would make him the highest-paid coach in college football (by $1) if he won a national championship.

That clause would soon come into effect.

6

BREAKTHROUGH IN THE BAYOU

Knowing these Tigers might contend for the national championship, Saban pushed the 2002 team harder than ever. His practices were intentionally frenetic, even stressful, to replicate the hurried, high-pressure atmosphere of a game. That way, after dozens of such practices players would get used to it and be calm when the real thing came. But Saban's approach was also part of a larger plan. "He was always breaking us down mentally, then building us back up,"[1] said quarterback Matt Mauck.

While it may seem as though patience was never Saban's strong suit, he showed at LSU and elsewhere that he would stand by troubled players so long as they were willing to change. "The worst thing was when we had a kid who got into trouble and wouldn't straighten out, and Coach had to kick him off the team," said defensive line coach

Pete Jenkins. "[Saban] would be hurt more than [ticked]."[2]

Defensive back Damien James was a key cog in Saban's defensive machine, an all-SEC performer and a leader during game time. But off the field, James got into trouble and Saban suspended him for the 2002 opener against Virginia Tech. James's absence was difficult to overcome and contributed to LSU losing the game. Saban worked out a "zero-tolerance contract" for James, and all was well until midseason, when he broke the conditions of the deal. Though no specifics were publicly given about how exactly James violated the contract, Saban felt that he had no choice but to dismiss his star from the team. "I absolutely knew I did the right thing," said Saban. "It was best for the program and for Damien. It set an example for the other players and, consequently, convinced them that their individual actions can be detrimental to the team."[3]

Spears Stayed Home

Marcus Spears was not only a first-team Class 1A All-State selection on both offense and defense, he was also a top basketball prospect. Though he hailed from Baton Rouge, it was still a coup for Nick Saban to land him in LSU's 2001 recruiting class. After a distinguished college career, Spears was selected by the Dallas Cowboys in the first round of the NFL Draft.

WIN FOR THE RIGHT REASONS

In the sixth game of the year, Mauck tore ligaments in his foot, and backup Marcus Randall was pressed into duty. Then came a game

LSU tailback Joseph Addai (#10) and the Tigers overcame multiple obstacles in the 2002 season, including this October loss to Auburn, but the most vital lesson they learned came at the end of the season.

remembered as one of the wildest, most improbable last-second comebacks ever. The underdog Kentucky Wildcats hosted LSU for what would be known as the "Bluegrass Miracle." The Tigers built a two-touchdown lead that the Wildcats chipped away at, finally tying the game at 27. Kentucky kicked a go-ahead field goal with eleven seconds left. LSU was pinned down at their own nine and, after one completion, found themselves seventy-four yards from the goal line with two seconds left on the clock.

The Wildcats didn't believe Randall had the arm to complete a Hail Mary heave that long and began celebrating. Their coach even got a Gatorade bath on the sideline. Then Randall's final throw, which did fall short of the end zone, resulted in a tipped ball caught by LSU receiver Devery Henderson at the fifteen-yard line. While Kentucky thought they'd won and their fans flooded the field, Henderson raced in for the game-winning score.

In general, Saban is always concerned when a team wins a game it should have lost because it makes it harder to fix the team's weaknesses. "When you play poorly and still win, that's the kiss of death," he said. "It doesn't send a good message. You have a lot of improving to do, but not the right frame of mind from which to accomplish it."[5]

> ***"When you play poorly and still win, that's the kiss of death."[4]***
>
> **—Nick Saban**

Sure enough, despite Saban's best efforts to prevent complacency in his team, the Tigers went into the next game overconfident and got shelled at home 31–0, courtesy of Alabama.

The team's last defeat of the year had the opposite effect, however. In the regular-season finale, LSU had a chance to win the SEC West once again and return to the SEC Championship. But they had to beat Arkansas first. With forty seconds to play it looked like the Tigers would do just that, leading 20–14. Then Razorbacks quarterback Matt Jones completed fifty- and thirty-yard passes to win by a single point. Given that the late breakdown in the secondary cost them the game, Saban was reminded of the price paid to punish Damien Jones and felt fairly certain the outcome would have been different had his star been back there. But the loss was a mixed blessing that Saban credits with compelling his players to focus as never before, laying the groundwork for greatness in 2003.

In a February meeting with his team, Saban asked everyone present to close their eyes and think about how they felt in the moments after the Arkansas loss. He didn't want anyone to forget it. They vowed to never be outworked again, not in the fourth quarter of a game or any day of the year. The coaches hit the road to recruit, and the players hit the weight room to work out. The players did these workouts voluntarily and in numbers, long before the official off-season conditioning program began. As a result, spring practices were more impressive than Saban could have hoped. There was no letup at any point along the way—everyone shared the same purpose and was fully committed to it.

Having taken Saban's teachings to heart, the seniors compiled a list of objectives for 2003. None of them had to do with the number of games won or championship hardware. One goal was to "Be a T.E.A.M.—Together Everyone Accomplishes More." Eliminating distractions was critical. Saban refers to distractions of any kind as "clutter," believing that thoughts of the past or future, larger goals or obstacles, simply undermine the effort to complete the task at hand to the best of one's ability. "Eliminate the clutter and all the

> *"It was then that the championship team was born."*[6]
>
> —Nick Saban

things that are going on outside, and focus on the things that you can control,"[7] he said.

It didn't hurt that LSU's 2003 recruiting class was the best in the nation that year, according to analysts. The Tigers had fourteen returning starters, four of them on the offensive line. Matt Mauck returned from his foot injury to lead the team, which came in fourteenth in the Associated Press's preseason poll.

Late in week two's blowout win over Arizona, television cameras captured Saban going ballistic on the sideline because his fourth-string running back had fumbled and it was returned for a touchdown. The play had no impact on the outcome of the game. "The thing you figure out about Nick real early is that it's fourth-and-one every second of every minute of every hour of every day,"[8] said Mike Collins, a member of Saban's staff at LSU. Saban's frequent sideline eruptions became legendary, thanks to the amused coverage of *SportsCenter* and other media.

TIGERS EARN THEIR STRIPES

In the middle of October, the Tigers were still undefeated and had ascended to ninth in the country, prompting BCS championship predictions. Then those predictions seemed foolish when they dropped a game to the Florida Gators, a potentially crippling blow to their chances. On the team, no one pointed fingers at each other, and Saban said, "The sun's gonna come up, I'm not going to fire anybody, let's get to work."[9]

Rumors swirled, suggesting that the Chicago Bears were courting Saban. At a speaking engagement he said, "It comes down to this: Do you want to deal with a bunch of immature people, or a bunch of college kids?"[10] The quote would soon be taken as proof of Saban's fickle nature, but over the longer term it became clear that he meant what he said.

THE SOONERS AND THE SUGAR BOWL

Though Saban is known as a defensively minded coach, the 2003 Tigers scored a school-record 475 points and averaged almost 34 per game. LSU closed out their schedule with a six-game winning streak. Every week someone else stepped up, supporting Saban's belief that teamwork is more important than talent. In the SEC Championship, LSU crushed Georgia 34–13. Their title aspirations got an assist when the previously undefeated Oklahoma Sooners were blown out in the Big 12 title game. Another one-loss team, USC, won its last game so the AP and coaches' polls had USC first, followed by LSU and Oklahoma. The BCS computers kept the Sooners in the top spot and ranked LSU

Summer Scare

During the July 4 weekend of 2003, Saban was vacationing with his family in the Georgia mountains. He slipped on his boat, hit his head, and fell into the lake, unconscious. Fortunately, he awoke at the lake bottom. "I came out of the accident with twenty-five stitches and a life lesson: never take anything for granted," said Saban. "We all seem to take things for granted when we don't buckle our seat belts or we drive too fast on a highway … Cherish your family and friends, for you never know when they, or you, will be taken away."[11]

second. This outcome meant that LSU would play Oklahoma in the Sugar Bowl with the BCS National Championship on the line.

Favored by 6.5 points, the Sooners had the 2003 Heisman Trophy winner in quarterback Jason White, along with head coach Bob Stoops, a lovable leader who insisted that his assistants spend quality time with their children. The unsmiling slave driver, Nick Saban, was cast as the villain in this overdramatic confrontation.

The Tigers came to play. At halftime, the Sooners' heralded offense had mustered just thirty-two yards and LSU clung to a 14–7 lead. Still, Saban challenged his best player on defense, Marcus Spears, in the locker room. "He said he needed me to figure out how I was

After his team topped Georgia 34–13 in the 2003 SEC title game, Saban endured the first of two icy Gatorade baths he would get that season.

going to affect this game, that I was a Baton Rouge kid, and that this was the biggest game of my life,"[12] said Spears.

Spears listened to his coach's call to action. On Oklahoma's first two offensive possessions of the second half, he sacked White and ran back an interception for a touchdown. Expecting his head coach to be thrilled, Spears trotted to the sidelines. "Instead, he just said, 'All right, I need you to go out and do a couple more things like that.'"[13]

In the fourth quarter, Oklahoma turned a Mauck interception into a touchdown to cut LSU's lead to 21–14 with eleven minutes to go in the game. Again, there was no sense of panic among the Tigers. They maintained their composure, the defense held firm, and with less than two minutes to go sacked White on fourth down to regain possession of the football. Oklahoma had no timeouts left, so all LSU had to do was run out the clock. However, on consecutive plays Mauck failed to milk the clock and lost yardage. Saban was furious and let his staff know it. "That was not a very pleasant time on the headset,"[14] noted offensive line coach Stacy Searels.

LSU had to punt with seven seconds left. Oklahoma brought the house and for a moment Saban feared the worst. But Donnie Jones, an excellent punter, got it away and soon the Tigers could celebrate. Saban found his seventeen-year-old son, Nicholas, and they embraced. Terry and their daughter, Kristen, would soon join them. If for only a moment, Saban could savor the thrill of victory. He knew Big Nick would be proud.

7

FLOUNDERING WITH THE FISH

Saban's moment of bliss was short-lived. In his postgame press conference he said, "This year's accomplishments are next year's expectations."[1] He was already feeling the pressure to defend the championship he'd won less than an hour earlier.

Perhaps to avoid those expectations, Saban was eyeing the NFL again. The Chicago Bears were back and doing their best to lure him to the Windy City. Saban didn't immediately sign a seven-year, $18.45-million deal to stay at LSU, at the time the largest deal ever offered to a college football coach. After the obligatory soul-searching, Saban stayed with the Tigers.

The 2004 recruiting class was rich in talent and ranked No. 2 in the country. The Tigers came in third in the preseason polls. Still, Saban caught a whiff of complacency from the defending champions. He also had to replace Mauck, who had graduated. In the season opener, LSU won a squeaker versus Oregon State, but the new quarterbacks struggled. The fans booed them and the media questioned their readiness, prompting an impassioned defense from Saban. He attributed the criticism to unrealistic expectations.

> *"This year's accomplishments are next year's expectations."*[2]
>
> **—Nick Saban**

LSU beat Arkansas State but then lost a 10–9 heartbreaker to Auburn in the annual Iron Bowl, meaning there was no margin for error if they were to mount a title defense. After thrashing Mississippi State, they lost to Georgia and any hopes of becoming back-to-back champs were dashed. In a postgame presser, Saban seemed completely blindsided by the outcome.

Saban's serenity seemed to unravel. He worried aloud about his parenting in a press conference. Word got out that charismatic Miami Dolphins owner Wayne Huizenga wanted to hire him. Asked by a Miami newspaper what his intentions were, Saban answered, "I'm happy here and my family is happy

In 2004, Saban elected to make the leap to the NFL and coach the Miami Dolphins.

here. I don't know anything about any other jobs."[3] LSU won its last three games and finished 9–2. Given the expectations Saban chafed against, that perfectly respectable record felt like losing six games—for him, the team, fans, and the media.

A MOVE TO THE NFL

The Dolphins' courtship continued. Saban admired Huizenga, a self-made millionaire. With Bill Belichick and the division rival Patriots coming off their third Super Bowl win in four years, Huizenga liked that Saban was Belichick's distinguished protégé and hoped the student was ready to surpass his teacher. In Miami, Saban could have near-total control over personnel, scouting, the draft, and the coaching staff.

Though the ink had scarcely dried on Saban's latest contract redo, he made the decision to walk away from LSU and accept his first NFL head-coaching job. He signed a five-year, $22.5-million deal with the Dolphins. "By that time it was starting to get

This Former Gator Flopped in Washington

With Florida, Steve Spurrier won six SEC championships in the 1990s and 2000. His Gators were national champions in 1996. The NFL presented another mountain to climb, however, and in 2002 Spurrier became the Washington Redskins' head coach. At the time, his five-year, $25-million contract was the most lucrative in league history. After 7–9 and 5–11 seasons, Spurrier quit. He later cited his struggles with the team's ownership as the main reason for their lack of success. Spurrier soon returned to the college ranks, coaching the South Carolina Gamecocks to an 86–49 record and five bowl wins.

aggravating," said LSU trustee Charlie Weems. "He's such a complicated guy, it's hard to know why he does it. He was the king of Louisiana at the time."[4]

Saban certainly left the program better than he'd found it. When Saban was hired in 1999, the team had forty-seven players with GPAs under 2.0. When he left, only three players fell below that threshold. Saban's recruits were an essential part of the 2007 team that won a national title in Les Miles's third season as his successor. Seventeen starters that year, including ten of the team's eleven defensive starters, were Saban recruits.

The NFL had continued to evolve since Saban's last stint in the league. Free agency had further empowered the players, and proven veterans were even more impervious to intimidation. After finishing a lowly 4–12 in 2004, Miami had little to speak of at the most critical position in football: quarterback.

Despite Saban's close ties to Bill Belichick, he couldn't exactly consult a division rival on making the adjustment to the pro game. He was on his own. Saban took it upon himself to know everything that was going on with the team—defense, offense, special teams—and to know it better than anyone.

The magnitude of the task at hand caused Saban a lot of stress, which made him curt with staffers. He was already known for walking by people in the hallway without acknowledging them—something his father might do—but Saban took it one step further in Miami. He never took the time to chat with anyone and reportedly

Saban's tenure in Miami was marked by frustration, an emotion he vented on the field.

blew up at a young staffer for getting the wrong kind of Little Debbie cakes, his favorite snack. A local news station captured footage of "the Nicktator" driving a rookie to tears at practice.

Despite it all, Saban coaxed the Dolphins to a 9–7 record and a second-place finish, defying expectations for a team expected to finish at the very bottom. Miami closed the year on a six-game winning streak. Saban's initially distrustful players appreciated the way he welcomed running back Ricky Williams back to the team. The enigmatic star had been banished for his marijuana usage, but the ever-forgiving Saban saw in Williams another opportunity to mentor a talented player with problems. Though Williams responded with a strong season, in the 2006 offseason he failed another drug test and was suspended for the year. Still, Saban stuck up for him.

WHO WOULD LEAD THEM?

The quarterback position remained a sore spot, but there were two potential solutions available: San Diego Charger Drew Brees, then a free agent, and Daunte Culpepper, a Minnesota Viking available via trade. Both were recuperating from serious injuries, but Culpepper was further along in his rehab. Saban preferred Brees, and they agreed to contract terms. Then Brees failed a physical with Miami's team doctors, which killed the deal. Given that Culpepper's recovery was more straightforward, acquiring him seemed like the best move at the time.

History would suggest otherwise. Brees went on to have a brilliant, Hall of Fame–worthy career with the New Orleans Saints, beginning with a 2006 appearance in the NFC Championship. As a Dolphin, Culpepper never regained his prior form. Such decisions have heavy consequences in the NFL, with bad deals often putting teams in "salary cap hell" for more than one season as they max out their budget paying for a disappointing player. Conversely, if one heralded recruit fizzles in college football, the outcome is quite different: another is often there waiting for his turn—especially when a coach has the recruiting prowess of Nick Saban.

Saban noticed that Culpepper seemed tentative on his bad knee, and there was no noticeable improvement as time went on. But the outside world saw Culpepper as a big upgrade, and both *Sports Illustrated* and *ESPN The Magazine* picked Miami to go to the Super Bowl. Then the Dolphins lost to Pittsburgh in the season opener, and Culpepper's lack of mobility was made clear. His failures on the field sealed a 28–17 loss.

Despite the slow start, the locker room remained in Saban's corner. Players admired his fiery personality, strategic mind, and smash-mouth style of football. His defensive schemes were as confusing to NFL passers as college players. Under Saban's tutelage, Jason Taylor had a phenomenal season and was named AP Defensive Player of the Year in 2006. On the offensive side, receiver Chris Chambers credits his only Pro Bowl season to Saban's coaching. "He put it all on my shoulders," said Chambers. "He took me to another level."[5]

Saban had also impressed the players with off-field innovations designed to improve their health: he arranged martial arts training in the off-season, hired a nutritionist, and minimized hitting in practice. A few years later the NFL would follow Saban's lead, limiting contact in practice by rule. Preventing head injuries remains a priority for Saban. At Alabama, Saban's current team, two team doctors evaluate all potential head injuries and decide whether or not the player can return to the field. It is never a coaching decision.

Daunte Culpepper was a force when he played for Minnesota, but a serious knee injury put his career in steep decline.

Entering the first of two annual showdowns with Bill Belichick and the Patriots, the Dolphins were 1–3. Saban thought that Culpepper's

8

RISING TIDE

Despite accepting a pay cut to coach the Crimson Tide, Saban would wield much more power at Alabama than he had in Miami. "In college, you are the GM, coach and head recruiter," he said. "You can develop and do more things to impact your future and control your destiny."[1] Conversely, professional football is much more tightly controlled and restricted. An NFL team's draft capital, salary-cap status, and incentive-laden contracts work to level the playing field and keep one team from unfairly dominating the sport year after year. The league wants fans in every city to feel they have a chance to win the Super Bowl, rather than allowing talent to be concentrated on the rosters of the best-run teams. Saban loathed this enforced mediocrity.

In the wake of Saban's departure, the Miami news coverage was savage. The *Herald* called him a loser and a weasel. Other derisive labels included "Tricky Nicky," "Nick $aban," "Nick Satan," and simply, "liar." Longtime Dolphins coach Don Shula told a newspaper, "he has

At Alabama, Saban found a home and the power to mold a program in his own image, from top to bottom.

run away from a challenge."[2] Of course, Saban was replacing Shula's son at Alabama. Meanwhile, there was evidence that Saban had wrung all he could have out of the Dolphins' roster. Many of the same players went 1–15 the next year, with their lone win coming in overtime.

REFORMING ALABAMA

Alabama looked like another rescue mission. With the exception of one national title under Gene Stallings, the program largely lay in ruins since its legendary coach, Bear Bryant, retired in 1982. "He is not trying to be the next Bear Bryant," said West Virginia senator Joe Manchin, a childhood friend. "He's going to be the first Nick Saban."[3]

Saban was the Tide's sixth coach in eight years, a span in which the team went 51–55 and won one bowl game in five tries. The school, boosters, and fans were desperate for their fortunes to change. Consequently, the university gave their new football coach unprecedented power over the program. Saban immediately got to work reshaping it in his image. John Parker Wilson, Alabama's starting QB in 2007 and 2008, said, "Everybody knew his direction, from the coaches down to the cafeteria staff."[4]

Saban expects the best from everyone down to groundskeepers and "gofers." Game-winning drives and everyday tasks should be treated with the same seriousness. "Leaders cannot accept mediocrity, as it impacts the culture of the organization,"[5] he proclaimed in his book.

Lonny Rosen remained a key consultant and counselor to Saban and to his players. "Fourth Quarter" practitioner Scott Cochran was hired as the team's strength and conditioning coach. Saban brought on a gaggle of unofficial coaches and consultants to assist in on-campus recruiting, scouting, and practice sessions. Nutritionists tailored the team's meals based on the demands of different positions. If players complained about the food, the menu changed. Saban instructed his staff to organize the players' lives and shield them from the distractions and temptations encountered outside the white lines.

Saban had taken The Process to the next level—he had each member of a large organization narrowly focused on his own small part of the big picture. Roles were sharply defined. He told players not to think about lifting a trophy at the end of the season. They should dedicate themselves to their conditioning, practice reps, and grades. His advice remains to control what you can control and find fulfillment in doing the work well. "Saban is the ultimate 'journey' man, and not a destination one,"[6] wrote his biographer, Monte Burke.

Once he had his players on the field, Saban put them through grueling practices no one was used to. The soft team he'd inherited would toughen up in a hurry. Saban changed their mindset and whipped their bodies into shape.

When it was time to play the games, Alabama raced out to a 5–2 start of the season. Then they faced Saban's former team—LSU had more of his recruits than the Tide did—in what some called the Saban Bowl. Alabama lost a dogfight, and it seemed to put the team into a tailspin. After losses to Mississippi State and Louisiana Monroe, who were twenty-five-point underdogs, Saban drew parallels to Pearl Harbor and 9/11. The point he was making was that "catastrophic events" can bring out the best in a group of people, but while, in relative terms, Alabama losing to Louisiana Monroe might be called catastrophic, his careless words were not well received.

> ***"He is not trying to be the next Bear Bryant. He's going to be the first Nick Saban."[7]***
>
> **—Joe Manchin**

Alabama squeaked into a bowl game and finished 7–6. Saban's old team, LSU, won the national title that year. It didn't bother him, as he was entirely focused on turning the Tide into champions. Saban

This Coach Cast a Long Shadow

Under Paul "Bear" Bryant, Alabama won six national championships. In 1983, he retired with more wins (323) than any coach in collegiate football history up to that point. With his six-foot-three (192-cm) frame and trademark houndstooth hat, Bryant cut a striking figure on the sideline. Bryant coached transcendent talents such as Joe Namath, Kenny Stabler, Ozzie Newsome, and John Hannah in the course of his twenty-five-year tenure in Tuscaloosa. "I don't want ordinary people," Bryant once said. "I want people who are willing to sacrifice and do without a lot of those things ordinary students get to do. That's what it takes to win."[8]

had developed a grading system that was a mix of what he'd learned under Don James and Bill Belichick, and his next recruiting class was filled with top talent. By this time Saban had earned the moniker "the Lord of the Living Room" for his persuasiveness and success in recruiting visits. His haul was particularly impressive considering that Saban had gone 22–23 since leaving LSU and that most of the publicity he received was negative. Rival coaches could always tell recruits, "He lied about Miami, and he'll lie about Alabama, too!"

YOUNG LEGS

Though the centerpiece of the 2008 recruiting class was receiver Julio Jones, a bona fide superstar, Saban also enticed a number of future NFL mainstays to sign letters of intent, including Mark Barron, Terrence Cody, Marcell Dareus, Dont'a Hightower, Mark Ingram, and Courtney Upshaw. Ingram, Hightower, and Upshaw weren't hotly contested recruits, but they proved to be diamonds in the rough. Saban lost out on generational talent Andrew Luck, who chose Stanford, but beyond this intriguing "what if?" moment he generally got what he wanted.

The Mobile, Alabama, area has produced a disproportionate number of prep stars, so Saban made it a point of emphasis. To lead the recruiting effort there, Saban turned to Lance Thompson, his linebacker coach and an excellent recruiter for Saban at LSU. Thompson softened them up with his easygoing charm, then the businesslike Saban closed the deal with talk about grades, becoming a man, and life after football. They would get the area players together and encourage their friendships. When one athlete committed to Alabama, it became much more likely that others would follow.

It was often essential to enlist the support of a recruit's mother, and that was certainly true in the case of Julio Jones. Fortunately, Jones's mother, Queen Marvin, was enamored with Saban. She liked that he insisted playing time must be earned, despite Jones's status as a five-star

Lord of the Living Room

Though Saban sometimes cracked jokes to show kids his human side, he generally projected a formal image when recruiting. Often wearing a nice suit, Saban would offer recruits a blueprint for personal success and a mission plan to execute. His businesslike attitude didn't mean that he employed doublespeak or jargon. Saban was blunt and straightforward and didn't promise playing time. But he made other commitments. According to Marcell Dareus, Saban said, "I promise you we're going to win; I promise you you'll get your degree; I promise you you'll become a better man than when you came in."[9]

Saban congratulates Florida's Urban Meyer after the Gators defeated the Crimson Tide in the 2008 SEC Championship game. Meyer is on the short list of coaches to have two wins over Saban's Alabama teams.

recruit. When the time came, her absurdly talented son would earn plenty of snaps.

Entering the 2008 campaign, Saban posted photos of the final scoreboards from the Mississippi State and Louisiana Monroe losses in the locker room and gym. No one would be allowed to forget them. Alabama won its opener 34–10 over Clemson, and right out of the gate Saban's new recruits played significant roles in the game. The freshmen were that talented and the roster was that thin.

By early November, Saban's undefeated team had ascended to the top spot in the BCS rankings. Making his return to Baton Rouge with the visiting team, Saban faced the extreme anger of his former fans. A scarecrow with Saban's face was burned in protest before the game, and the Alabama team was assigned a security detail of thirty-two police officers. The unfriendly atmosphere didn't undermine Alabama's effort, however, as the Crimson Tide won 27–21 in overtime. Later, they broke a six-game losing streak to Auburn with a major win, 36–0.

In the 2008 SEC Championship game, Alabama faced Urban Meyer's fearsome Florida Gators, who were ranked No. 2 in the country. Halfway through the fourth quarter, Alabama held a 20–17 lead. That's when Florida quarterback Tim Tebow took over, leading the Gators to a pair of touchdowns and a 31–20 win. The defeat marked Saban's only loss in a championship game up to that point. The Tide could take some small measure of consolation in the fact that Florida went on to win the national title.

Though the loss would sting for some time, this team was ready to take that last step and win it all.

9

THE BIG PAYOFF

While Lance Thompson left the program in early 2009, he first helped Alabama put together a top-flight recruiting class. Big names Trent Richardson, D. J. Fluker, and AJ McCarron were NFL-caliber talents. That year, Alabama opened its newly renamed visitors' locker room. Above the entrance were the prominent words "THE FAIL ROOM." Booster James M. Fail was responsible for this subtle act of psychological warfare, which pleased Saban greatly. "I figured it was the most appropriate opportunity I would ever have to use my name,"[1] explained Fail.

Entering year three of his rebuild, Saban welcomed the 2009 recruiting class to campus. By this point, a majority of the players were his recruits. Greg McElroy took over as the team's signal caller. He was a smart player and a natural leader. The team had an

The Sabans are extremely active in their community. Here, Terry speaks at the 2015 dedication ceremony for the Nick's Kids Playground in Tuscaloosa, Alabama.

embarrassment of riches in the backfield—Mark Ingram now had to fend off teammate Trent Richardson for touches. "We can be an outstanding team," Saban told his charges. "I'm not worried about the talent ... But how bad do you want it?"[2]

Nick's old friend Kerry Marbury said that Terry saw her husband only once a week that year and he forgot his wedding anniversary. She understood. Much warmer than Saban, Terry thrived in the role of the college coach's wife. "She became the smiling human face of the machinelike program,"[3] wrote Burke in his Saban biography. If

Saban didn't always acknowledge people, Terry would greet folks with hugs. She chatted with fans, delivered speeches, and organized fundraisers for student groups and Big Brothers Big Sisters. Terry was deeply involved in the Sabans' charity, Nick's Kids Foundation, which they started in the Michigan State days. Since its inception, the nonprofit has distributed more than $4 million.

The 2009 season opened with fifth-ranked Alabama playing seventh-ranked Virginia Tech. Mark Ingram ran roughshod over the Hokies, and the Tide prevailed, 34–24. They reeled off another six wins by an average score of 35–10. Tennessee gave Alabama a real tussle in Tuscaloosa, but defensive tackle Terrence Cody blocked his second kick of the day to secure a 12–10 win. From there it was mostly clear sailing for the Tide, who concluded their second straight year with an unblemished 12–0 regular-season mark. Ingram became the first Alabama player to win the Heisman Trophy.

> ***"You don't coach with him to have fun."[4]***
>
> **—Rob Sale**

POSTSEASON PROGRESS

The SEC Championship game presented a rematch with the Florida Gators. Urban Meyer's team was the top-ranked team in the country and had won two NCAA titles in the last three years. Tim Tebow had gone twenty-two consecutive games without a loss. Saban noticed that before kickoff, his team was eerily silent. There was no music playing in the locker room, no shouting or even talking. The Crimson Tide knew what they had to do to put the previous year's defeat behind them.

Alabama played their most fundamentally sound game of the season and won 32–13. Ingram scored three touchdowns, and Greg McElroy did a passable Tim Tebow impression. Saban's transformation of the program was complete.

Alabama advanced to play the 13–0 Texas Longhorns at the Rose Bowl in Pasadena, with the national championship at stake. In this game it was Marcell Dareus who stole the spotlight—and an errant pass. With Texas quarterback Colt McCoy injured, his freshman

Nick consoles Florida quarterback Tim Tebow after Alabama handed him his first loss in twenty-two games, defeating the defending national champions 32–13 to win the 2009 SEC title.

backup was intercepted by Dareus, who rumbled all the way to the end zone. In the end, Alabama completed a 14–0 season with a 37–21 win and Saban's second NCAA title. He became the first coach since Pop Warner to win national championships at two schools. Alabama was the first FBS team to defeat six schools ranked in the AP Top 25 during one season. They had certainly earned their trophy.

The next morning, Saban gathered his assistant coaches to begin preparations for the fall season. "There was still no joy in triumph,"[5] wrote Burke. Assistant Rob Sale said, "You don't coach with him to have fun. You do it if you want to win and be successful."[6]

AUBURNED

On paper, the 2010 team looked even stronger than the 2009 champions. Other than team leader Javier Arenas, most key contributors came back. All was well early as the Tide won their first five games, including a 31–6 triumph over Florida to notch their twenty-ninth straight "W." Saban noticed that the sideline seemed too casual, though—the team was coasting. The streak came to an end the next week when Steve Spurrier's South Carolina Gamecocks handed Alabama a 35–21 loss. This rare defeat frustrated Saban tremendously because of the root causes. Still in the thick of the race, Alabama visited Baton Rouge with a 7–1 record. They were up 14–10 in the final quarter. But it wasn't to be, as LSU pulled out a 24–21 win. The next, even more devastating setback came when Alabama played an 11–0 Auburn team led by a linebacker-sized dual-threat quarterback: Cam Newton. Though the Tide jumped out to a 24–0 advantage in the second quarter, Newton led a huge comeback in the second half and Auburn limited Alabama to sixty-seven total yards after intermission. The final score was 28–27, Auburn.

The tone changed when Alabama blew out Michigan State in the Capital One Bowl, as Saban thought his team finally played up to its potential. He felt confident that the players returning in 2011 were committed.

The 2011 "Super Outbreak"

In April 2011, a host of highly destructive tornadoes ravaged the United States, doing the most damage in Alabama and Mississippi. The death toll included 254 Alabama residents, six of them students at Saban's university. One of the victims was Ashley Harrison, whose boyfriend Carson Tinker played for the Tide. The Sabans donated $75,000 to tornado relief through Nick's Kids Foundation. In the disaster's aftermath, Saban handed out Gatorade, thanked relief workers, and spoke at a memorial for the deceased students.

Though each season yielded a rich bounty of fresh talent in Tuscaloosa, the Lord of the Living Room didn't land every recruit. Defensive end Jadeveon Clowney wasn't feeling it with Saban or his defensive scheme. Quarterback James Winston liked the coach but felt that he could be himself at Florida State. Both players would later be picked first overall in the NFL Draft.

The 2011 Tide had a stingy and effective defense, surrendering just eight points per game. As orchestrated by defensive coordinator Kirby Smart, Saban's second-longest-tenured assistant, the complex

Though losses have been rare in the Saban era, in November 2011 Alabama lost a defensive struggle to LSU, 9–6. The Crimson Tide avenged the defeat in the national title game.

scheme challenged players. "It's pretty much like an NFL program," said Mark Barron, now a linebacker for the Los Angeles Rams. "Well, actually, I know for a fact that it's more complicated than a lot of NFL systems. So just having to learn that and go through that whole process of putting in the work, the work that it takes to be successful at Alabama, that prepares you for the work you have to put in to come in and have success in the NFL."[7]

The only blemish on the season was LSU's visit to Bryant-Denny Stadium for the fifth Saban Bowl. While Alabama held LSU to nine points, they only scored six themselves in an overtime loss. After getting back on track, Alabama narrowly edged Oklahoma State in the

BCS rankings to earn a rematch with LSU, this time in the national championship. Saban's squad shut out the Tigers to claim a 21–0 win.

As usual, Saban called the team together for a meeting three days later. "That was a lot of fun," he said. "But now it's in the past."[8] For Saban there was never time to enjoy a win—he was already on to the next one.

10

THE DEFINITION OF DOMINANCE

In 2012, Saban was entering his sixth season with Alabama, making this his longest stop with any ball club. Had his wanderlust dissipated? Agent Jimmy Sexton got in touch with a few teams without it hitting the media. He wanted to make sure the administration knew his client was still in high demand. For seemingly the umpteenth time in his coaching career, Saban's contract was renegotiated. Lance Thompson returned, continuing another trend—Saban's assistants often leave and come back a few years later. Perhaps they need a break from the intensity of his team culture. In any case, it doesn't offend Saban, and he likes to give his players different voices to listen to.

The 2012 team was again ranked number one. But that didn't mean they didn't face any challengers. Texas A&M ran an up-tempo

Saban celebrates with his players after Alabama beat Georgia 32–28 in 2012 to secure his second conference title.

offense with quarterback Johnny Manziel. "Johnny Football" played the chaotic, schoolyard style of ball that Saban hates. Manziel engineered a 29–24 upset win at Bryant-Denny.

This proved a small speed bump to overcome. After the Tide edged Georgia in a thrilling SEC Championship game, 32–28, they found themselves back in the BCS Championship game. This time the opponent was an undefeated Notre Dame team. Practice during the week didn't meet Saban's high standards and he lit into his team. "After we watched the film, Coach Saban just let us have it," said defensive tackle Quinton Dial. “It was about as [ticked] as I’d seen him. He told us to get our minds right. We had two great practices after that. It got us ready.”[1]

The Tide led 28–0 at half and won 41–14, becoming the only team to win consecutive national championships since the BCS era began in 1998. The last team to do it? The mid-1990s Nebraska team Saban had long admired.

> ***“You win college football games in February, March and April, not just in the fall.”[2]***
>
> **—Nick Saban**

With this championship in hand, the heralded 2008 recruiting class graduated. They’d gone a jaw-dropping 61–7. After reaching the summit of college football two years in a row, Saban felt exhausted. But rather than getting a monkey off his back, he felt more pressure than ever to keep the good times rolling. Boosters and fans immediately began pondering the possibility of a “three-peat.”

PROVING HIS WORTH

Lacking 2012’s senior leadership, the Tide’s 2013 team had an entitled attitude that irritated Saban. He called them out in the press and suspended ten players for various transgressions. Though “The Process” seemed to be breaking down, the team’s winning ways continued. Practices got sloppier, and Saban couldn’t snap them out of it. The chickens came home to roost with “the Kick Six,” a disappointing season’s signature loss. In the 2013 Iron Bowl, Alabama controlled the game until the end. Auburn scored to tie it up, 28–28, with less than a minute left. The Tide got into position to attempt one last play, a fifty-seven-yard field goal attempt. The kick fell short, and Auburn returner Chris Davis blazed through Alabama's sluggish attempts to tackle him. His touchdown ended the game, 34–28.

With that, Saban's shot at a third straight national title came to an abrupt end. There was once again speculation about his next move. Terry told the *Wall Street Journal*, "You come to a crossroads and the expectations get so great, people get spoiled by success, and there starts to be a lack of appreciation. We're kind of there now."[3]

Jimmy Sexton always kept Saban's options open. Saban once told a newspaper that without his aggressive agent, "I don't think I'd ever make one change [of jobs], the way I am."[4] The coach was linked to another historically prominent program, the Texas Longhorns. For a man who would rather build a winning team than maintain it, it was an appealing possibility. The school had ample resources and a top-notch recruiting base in-state.

Alabama quelled the speculation by giving Saban a new deal. Not only was it the richest in college football, only three NFL coaches earned a larger paycheck in 2014. (According to Forbes in 2017, the school itself pays him little more than $250,000 while the rest is a "talent fee" paid by the Crimson Tide Foundation, which raises money through boosters and brand licensing.) "I think Nick is actually way underpaid,"[5] said Alabama trustee Angus Cooper. In 2016, the Alabama football team turned a $48-million profit and saw its revenues climb 10 percent in one year.[6] Enrollment has grown by fourteen thousand since Saban's arrival, and the university is actually much more selective with admissions today. "The year before Saban arrived, Alabama accepted 77% of its applicants," wrote Burke in *Forbes*. "It now admits just over 50%."[7]

Saban's group began the 2014 season 4–0 before Ole Miss tripped them up, 23–17. The team then embarked on an eight-game winning streak that included a hard-fought victory over LSU in Baton Rouge. Alabama also beat top-ranked Mississippi State. The next Iron Bowl went better, as the Tide came out on the winning side of a 55–44 shootout. Quarterback Blake Sims had played better than expected, and receiver Amari Cooper placed third in Heisman voting. In the SEC Championship game, Alabama thrashed Missouri 42–13.

By season's end the team was No. 1 and the top seed in the new College Football Playoff. In the national semifinal, an Ohio State team coached by Saban nemesis Urban Meyer knocked off the Tide. This incarnation of his team still pleased Saban,

A Star Receiver

Amari Cooper had a season for the ages in 2014. With 124 receptions for 1,727 yards and 16 touchdowns, he set numerous single-season school records versus top-drawer defenses. He was the first Alabama player, and the second in SEC history, to win the Biletnikoff Award as the nation's top receiver. Cooper also became Alabama's all-time leader in receptions (229), receiving yards (3,463), and receiving touchdowns (31). In 2015 the Oakland Raiders made him the fourth overall selection in the NFL Draft, and he was selected to the Pro Bowl in both of his first two seasons.

who saw them as overachievers. "This has been one of the most pleasurable teams we've had to coach,"[8] he said on his weekly radio show late in the year. Ohio State bested Oregon to win the national title. Combined, Meyer and Saban had won six of the last nine Division I championships.

CLEMSON CONFRONTATIONS WERE CLASSIC

There was gleeful talk of the death of a dynasty when, in 2015, the 2–0 Tide lost to Ole Miss 43–37, at home. But Saban reminded his players of the twenty-four-hour rule that was a central tenet of his Process:

The Crimson Tide's triumph over the Clemson Tigers in the 2016 College Football Playoff National Championship Game coaxed a big smile out of the normally stoic Saban.

once it's over, win or lose, it's time to move on. Saban's team did just that, winning their next nine games. Along the way they handed a 38–10 defeat to the previously undefeated, and favored, Georgia Bulldogs. Saban would later say this was his favorite team to coach. They won with a smothering defense, punishing running game, and mistake-free quarterback play. The team featured 2015 Heisman winner Derrick Henry, who shattered Herschel Walker's thirty-four-year-old SEC record for most rushing yards in a single season.

Entering the College Football Playoff, Alabama trounced Michigan State in a shutout before facing the Clemson Tigers. Saban had assembled sixty-six recruits with four- or five-star status, to thirty-seven on the other side. Under the bright lights, his star players came through. Henry had a trio of touchdowns, and tight end O. J. Howard rolled up 208 receiving yards and a pair of scores.

One would think that Alabama won easily, with such an impressive offensive output. But they were up against Deshaun Watson, a quarterback with the mobility and improvisational flair that gives Saban's defenses fits. No one in history had gained more total yards in a national championship game than the Heisman finalist's 478 that night. The fact that Watson did it against the third-ranked defense in the nation was all the more eye-opening.

The Tide trailed by three in the fourth quarter. After a successful field goal, Saban attempted a surprise onside kick. Though he'd had his players practice this all season, it was a move many gamblers would second-guess. The Tide lined up like normal, but kicker Adam

Griffith perfectly executed a short bounce that was recovered by a teammate. Alabama took advantage of this unexpected drive to score a touchdown and went on to win 45–40.

Saban's gutsy call paid off partially because it was so out of character. With the 2015 national championship added to his collection, every one of Saban's Alabama recruiting classes had won one. Less than a month later, he signed the consensus No. 1 recruiting class in the country. Again. The talent will always be there, if not experience, as many star players skip their senior seasons to go pro. In part, elite recruits choose 'Bama because they want to reach the NFL someday.

> ***"Dominance may emerge from the physical, but it becomes a psychological weapon."*[9]**
>
> **—Nick Saban**

While Clemson would come out on top in the teams' national championship rematch in January 2017, with Watson leading the Tigers to a last-second 35–31 win, the Tide rolls on. It seems highly unlikely that Saban's trophy tally will be stuck on five for long. The question is, will his next title be won at Alabama? Most likely, but Saban doesn't regret his nomadic career path. "Moving from place to place was hard for my family and for me because of the loyalty factor that my parents and coaches had taught me early on," Saban conceded in his book. "But I do believe that everything happens for a purpose, and every stop along the way in my professional journey helped me become a better coach and a better person."[10]

Share the Wealth?

College football is a huge moneymaker, and it's made coaches like Nick Saban millionaires. And yet the NCAA forbids athletes from receiving compensation for making that multibillion-dollar industry possible. (They do get "swag" during bowl season, much of it electronics.) "We can't pay them, but we can reinvest in trying to help them be successful in their future,"[13] Saban said in 2014. That's especially important given the enormous commitment of time and energy playing for a team like Alabama requires. Many players come from low-income families and leave school early because of the pressure to provide for their loved ones.

Through the 2017–18 season Alabama under Saban had posted a 132–20 record, winning 87 percent of its games. In the 2018 national championship game, Saban's decision to start backup quarterback Tua Tagovailoa in the second half proved to be a masterstroke, as the true freshman engineered a comeback to edge Georgia in overtime and give Saban his sixth NCAA title, tying Bear Bryant's record.

In addition to his NCAA titles, Saban has won seven SEC championships. "I remain fascinated by Saban," wrote Don Yaeger, author of *Great Teams: 16 Things High Performing Organizations Do Differently*. "Love him or hate him (and most find themselves in the second camp), Saban embodies Greatness."[11]

Dominance can be defined as an overwhelming superiority that is almost impossible to stop. It's a subject Saban has done a lot of thinking about. "Develop an attitude that you simply cannot be

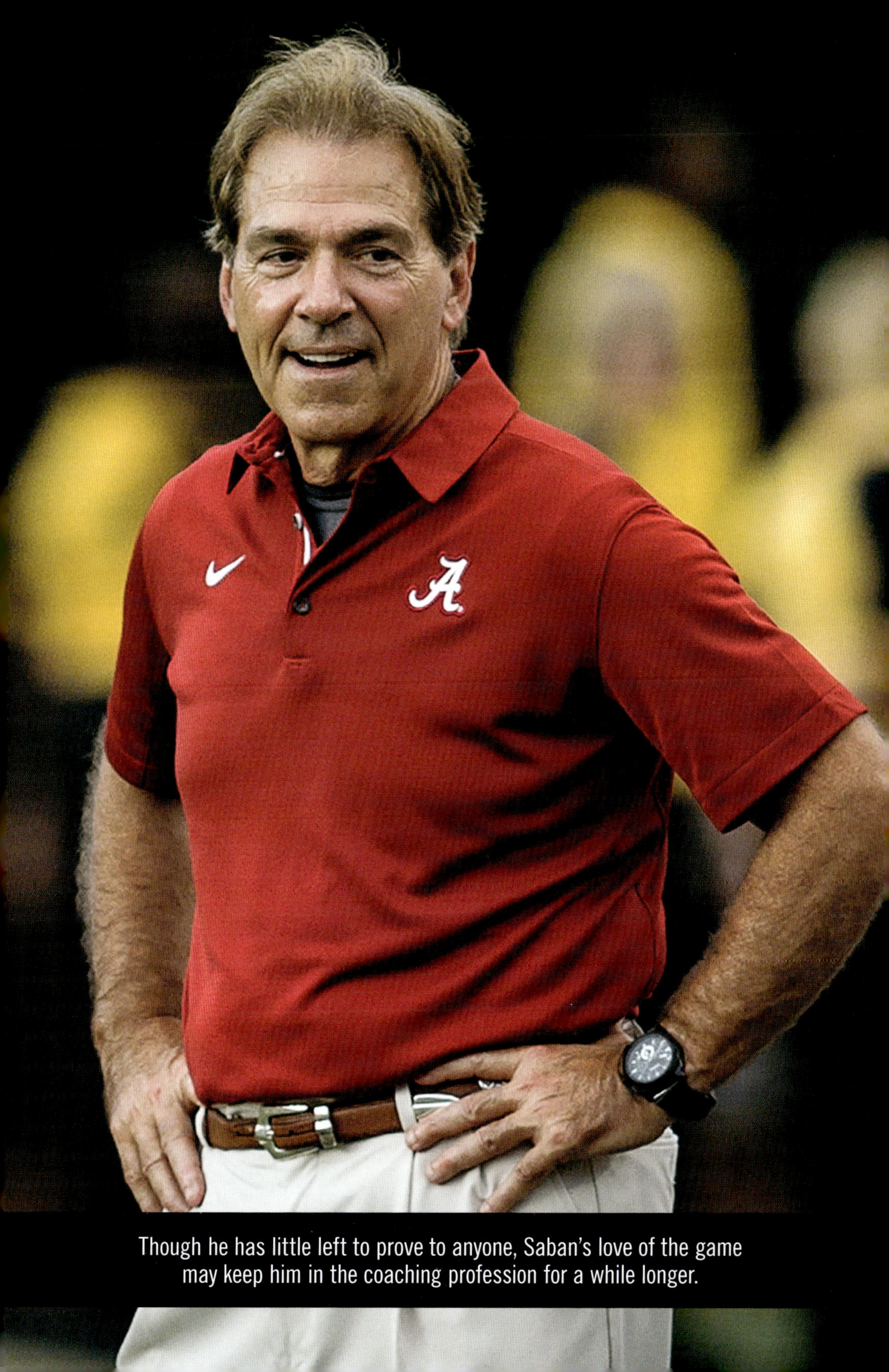

Though he has little left to prove to anyone, Saban's love of the game may keep him in the coaching profession for a while longer.

beaten—that you are an overpowering force," Saban advised in his book. "You may be surprised by how positive thinking impacts your performance."[12]

In Saban's eyes, what makes a team (or individual) dominant are the drive to win, the relentless pursuit of perfection, and the toughness to weather adversity. In his book, he suggested that these qualities can be applied to any project or goal or professional field, certainly in the business world.

WHAT'S NEXT?

When will Saban retire to the golf course or television analyst's chair? In May 2017 his salary got yet another bump, making him the highest-paid coach in American sports. From 2017 until 2025, Saban will receive a staggering $74.4 million in total compensation. But he's not in this for the money, not anymore. Saban's birthday falls on Halloween—his opponents would say playing him is definitely more trick than treat—and in 2018 he turned sixty-seven. He is now among the oldest coaches in major college football. These days you're more likely to see a smile on Saban's face, especially if he's asked about his granddaughter. His persona as a guest on ESPN is warm, self-deprecating, and generous. The mellowing process is well underway, and Saban has said he feels he owes it to Terry to bow out eventually.

On the other hand, Saban still loves what he does. His players have observed that he's happiest at practice, and his wife says he'd rather coach and watch film than do just about anything. And Saban believes that, in some small way, his work makes the world a better place. In his book, Saban recounted a dinner shared with the Reverend Jesse Jackson in Baton Rouge. Jackson remarked that, in a sense, Saban's team was closer to the Kingdom of God than his church. "I was stunned. He went on to explain that our squad is one of the places where rich and poor, black and white, share a common goal, the rules are clearly defined, and everyone has a chance to succeed. I was flattered and I would like to think this is true in every part of our program—academics included."[14]

Big Nick coached until the day he died, and one has to wonder if his son will ever willingly give up the game, either. Not having achieved true perfection yet, he still hears his father's voice in the back of his mind and remains driven to do it all over again until it's *right*.

CHRONOLOGY

1951 Nicholas Lou Saban Jr. is born in Fairmont, West Virginia.

1971 Nick and Terry Constable get married.

1973 Saban is hired as a graduate assistant at his alma mater, Kent State.

1978 The West Virginia Mountaineers make Saban their secondary coach.

1980 Saban is hired to coach the Ohio State Buckeyes' defensive backs.

1983 The Michigan State Spartans bring on Saban to coordinate their defense.

1988 Saban joins the staff of the NFL's Houston Oilers, as secondary coach.

1990 The Toledo Rockets give Saban his first head-coaching job.

1991 Bill Belichick brings Saban back to the NFL, where he becomes the Cleveland Browns' defensive coordinator.

1994 In Cleveland, Saban's defense surrenders just 204 points, best in the league.

1995 Saban becomes the head coach of the Michigan State Spartans.

1998 Nick and Terry establish the Nick's Kids Foundation in honor of his father.

2000 The LSU Tigers lure Saban away from Michigan State.

2003 LSU defeats the Oklahoma Sooners in the BCS Championship game, winning Saban's first national title. Saban is voted AP Coach of the Year.

2005 Wayne Huizenga hires Saban to be the head coach of the Miami Dolphins.

2006 In Miami, Saban suffers his only losing season as a head coach (6–10).

2007 Saban takes over the Alabama Crimson Tide.

2008 The Associated Press recognizes Saban with Coach of the Year honors.

2009 Alabama knocks off the Texas Longhorns, 37–21, to finish 14–0 and secure Saban's second NCAA title.

2011 The Crimson Tide shuts out Saban's old team, the LSU Tigers, 21–0, delivering Alabama's fourteenth national championship.

2012 Saban wins his fourth NCAA title in four years when Alabama defeats the Notre Dame Fighting Irish, 42–14.

2015 Alabama edges the unbeaten, No. 1–ranked Clemson Tigers 45–40 to claim Saban's fifth national title.

2016 The Tide lose their national championship rematch with Clemson, 35–31, on Deshaun Watson's game-winning TD pass with one second left.

2018 Facing off against the Georgia Bulldogs, the Tide is victorious, delivering Nick Saban's sixth NCAA title, tying Bear Bryant's legendary record.

http://www.al.com/alabamafootball/index.ssf/2014/10/alabama_coach_nick_saban_opens.html.
9. Burke, p. 50.
10. Saban and Curtis, p. 21.
11. Burke, p. 62.
12. Saban and Curtis, p. 209.
13. Burke, p. 63.
14. Ibid., p. 67.

CHAPTER 3: MAKE A DIFFERENCE AND MOVE ON

1. Monte Burke, *The Making of a Coach* (New York, NY: Simon & Schuster, 2015), p. 71.
2. Nick Saban and Brian Curtis, *How Good Do You Want to Be?* (New York, NY: Ballantine Books, 2005), p. 210.
3. Ibid., p. 198.
4. Burke, p. 75.
5. Saban and Curtis, p. 67.
6. Ibid., p. 96.
7. Ibid., p. 75.
8. Burke, p. 91.
9. Nickel, Brandon, "Alabama Football: Nick Saban Does not 'believe in tired,'" *Bama Hammer*, October 20, 2017, https://bamahammer.com/2017/10/20/alabama-football-nick-saban-not-believe-tired/.

10. Henry McKenna, "Dont'a Hightower on Playing for Both Nick Saban, Bill Belichick: 'It's Been Hell,'" PatriotsWire.com, September 4, 2017, http://patriotswire.usatoday.com/2017/09/04/donta-hightower-on-playing-for-both-nick-saban-bill-belichick-its-been-hell/.
11. Saban and Curtis, p. 66.

CHAPTER 4: FLIRTATIONS AND FORMIDABLE TEAMS

1. Monte Burke, *The Making of a Coach* (New York, NY: Simon & Schuster, 2015), p. 98.
2. Nick Saban and Brian Curtis, *How Good Do You Want to Be?* (New York, NY: Ballantine Books, 2005), p. 70.
3. Burke, p. 98.
4. Chris Vannini, "Saban: I Remember Tom Osborne Telling Me You're not as Bad as You Think," CoachingSearch.com, January 13, 2016, http://coachingsearch.com/article?a=Nick-Saban-I-remember-Tom-Osborne-telling-me-youre-not-as-bad-as-you-think.
5. Saban and Curtis, p. 29.
6. Burke, p. 116.
7. Vannini.
8. Ibid.
9. Monte Burke, "The Most Powerful Coach in Sports," *Forbes*, August 14, 2008, https://www.forbes.com/forbes/2008/0901/092.html.

10. Seth Davis, "Q&A: SMU Coach Larry Brown Discusses His Storied Career," SI.com, December 1, 2014, https://www.si.com/college-basketball/2014/12/01/larry-brown-interview-smu-mustangs.
11. Burke, p. 126.
12. Saban and Curtis, p. 67.
13. Kyle Austin, "Nick Saban: Michigan State Still Seems like Home, 17 Years After Leaving," MLive.com, January 9, 2017, http://www.mlive.com/spartans/index.ssf/2017/01/nick_saban_michigan_state_stil.html.

CHAPTER 5: PROCESS DRIVEN

1. Warren St. John, "Nick Saban: Sympathy for the Devil," GQ.com, August 25, 2013, https://www.gq.com/story/coach-nick-saban-alabama-maniac.
2. Nick Saban and Brian Curtis, *How Good Do You Want to Be?* (New York, NY: Ballantine Books, 2005), p. 145.
3. Monte Burke, *The Making of a Coach* (New York, NY: Simon & Schuster, 2015), p. 147.
4. Ibid., p. 154.
5. Ibid., p. 130.
6. Ibid.
7. Saban and Curtis, p. 161.
8. Ibid., p. 138.

9. Burke, p. 165.
10. Ibid., p. 166.

CHAPTER 6: BREAKTHROUGH IN THE BAYOU

1. Monte Burke, *The Making of a Coach* (New York, NY: Simon & Schuster, 2015), p. 168.
2. Ibid., p. 164.
3. Nick Saban and Brian Curtis, *How Good Do You Want to Be?* (New York, NY: Ballantine Books, 2005), p. 190.
4. Ibid., p. 71.
5. Ibid.
6. Ibid., p. 5.
7. Greg Bishop, "Saban Is Keen To Explain Process," *New York Times*, January 5, 2013, https://thequad.blogs.nytimes.com/2013/01/05/saban-is-keen-to-explain-process/.
8. Burke, p. 174.
9. Ibid., p. 175.
10. Ibid., p. 174.
11. Saban and Curtis, p. 203.
12. Burke, p. 177.
13. Ibid., p. 178.
14. Ibid.

CHAPTER 7: FLOUNDERING WITH THE FISH

1. Monte Burke, *The Making of a Coach* (New York, NY: Simon & Schuster, 2015), p. 179.
2. Ibid.
3. Ibid., p. 184.
4. Ibid., p. 185.
5. Ibid., p. 209.
6. Ibid., p. 212.
7. Ibid., p. 217.
8. Emily Kaplan, "Saban Says," *Sports Illustrated*, August 31, 2016, https://www.si.com/mmqb/2016/08/31/nick-saban-ncaa-college-football-alabama-nfl-draft-concussions.

CHAPTER 8: RISING TIDE

1. Monte Burke, *The Making of a Coach* (New York, NY: Simon & Schuster, 2015), p. 218.
2. Ibid.
3. Paul Gattis, "Retro Edition: Looking Back at Nick Saban's West Virginia Roots," AL.com, December 21, 2009, http://blog.al.com/chatter/2009/12/retro_edition_looking_back_at.html.
4. Burke, p. 225.
5. Nick Saban and Brian Curtis, *How Good Do You Want to Be?* (New York, NY: Ballantine Books, 2005), p. 140.
6. Burke, p. 231.

7. Gattis.
8. Mike Puma, "Bear Bryant 'Simply the Best There Ever Was,'" ESPN Classic, https://www.espn.com/classic/biography/s/Bryant_Bear.html.
9. Burke, p. 244.

CHAPTER 9: THE BIG PAYOFF

1. Monte Burke, *The Making of a Coach* (New York, NY: Simon & Schuster, 2015) p. 255.
2. Ibid.
3. Ibid., p. 256.
4. Ibid., p. 263.
5. Ibid.
6. Ibid.
7. Mark Inabinett, "Nick Saban's Defense 'More Complicated' than Some NFL Teams' Systems, Mark Barron says," AL.com, October 2, 2016, http://www.al.com/sports/index.ssf/2016/10/nick_sabans_defense_more_compl.html.
8. Don Yaeger, "What Nick Saban Taught Me About Greatness And Its Worst Nemesis: Complacency," *Forbes*, January 11, 2017, https://www.forbes.com/sites/donyaeger/2017/01/11/what-nick-saban-taught-me-about-greatness-and-its-worst-nemesis-complacency/#48cc81403986.

CHAPTER 10: THE DEFINITION OF DOMINANCE

1. Monte Burke, *The Making of a Coach* (New York, NY: Simon & Schuster, 2015) p. 289.
2. Nick Saban and Brian Curtis, *How Good Do You Want to Be?* (New York, NY: Ballantine Books, 2005), p. 71.
3. Burke, p. 303.
4. Ibid., p. 301.
5. Ibid., p. 309.
6. Michael Casagrande, "Alabama Football Brought in record $103.9 Million as Athletics Profit Jumps," AL.com, February 23, 2017, http://www.al.com/alabamafootball/index.ssf/2017/02/alabama_football_brought_in_10.html.
7. Monte Burke, "Nick Saban Will Make $11 Million Next Football Season and He Is Worth Every Penny," *Forbes*, May 2, 2017, https://www.forbes.com/sites/monteburke/2017/05/02/nick-saban-will-make-11-million-next-football-season-and-he-is-worth-every-penny/#5a2e3736403e.
8. Burke, *The Making of a Coach*, p. 323.
9. Saban and Curtis, p. 116.
10. Ibid., p. 212.
11. Don Yaeger, "What Nick Saban Taught Me About Greatness And Its Worst Nemesis: Complacency," *Forbes*, January 11, 2017, https://www.forbes.com/sites/donyaeger/2017/01/11/what-nick-saban-taught-me-about-greatness-and-its-worst-nemesis-complacency/#48cc81403986.

12. Saban and Curtis, p. 119.
13. Zac Ellis, "Alabama Coach Nick Saban: 'I've Always Been an Advocate of Players' Rights,'" *Sports Illustrated*, April 01, 2014, https://www.si.com/college-football/campus-union/2014/04/01/nick-saban-alabama-northwestern-union.
14. Saban and Curtis, p. 180.

GLOSSARY

anthracite A rare coal with few impurities that burns with little flame and smoke.

bulletin board material Actions or statements that could be perceived as disrespectful of a team's opponent, potentially motivating them to play harder.

conditioning The process of getting athletes into optimal shape for competition.

dual threat A quarterback who is as dangerous running the ball as throwing it.

FBS The NCAA Division I Football Bowl Subdivision (FBS) is the highest level of competition in college football.

field goal An attempt to score three points by kicking the football between the goalposts.

free agency The concept of players' eligibility, as free agents, to reach a contract agreement with any team they choose.

game plan The offensive and defensive strategies devised by a team in order to win a specific game.

Hail Mary A deep pass thrown with little or no time on the game clock, when completing this pass is essentially a team's last "prayer" of victory.

Heisman Trophy The most prestigious individual honor in college football, the Heisman is presented to the season's most outstanding player.

Iron Bowl The annual rivalry game between Alabama's two biggest football powers, the Crimson Tide and the Auburn Tigers.

onside kick A kickoff with the goal of retaining possession; the kick must travel at least ten yards before it can legally be recovered by the kicking team.

pick six An intercepted pass (also known as a "pick") that the defense returns for a touchdown, scoring six points.

prep In a football context, a high school athlete preparing to advance to the collegiate level.

presser Media slang for a press conference.

Pro Bowl The annual all-star game of the National Football League.

punt A kick that turns the football over to the other team, hopefully about forty yards from the line of scrimmage.

sack When a defender tackles a quarterback behind the line of scrimmage.

safety In this context, a member of the secondary who represents the last line of defense.

salary cap The limit the league puts on the amount of money that a team can spend on players' salaries.

scheme An offensive or defensive strategy developed by a team's coaching staff to coordinate players' efforts on the field.

secondary The group of defensive backs lining up behind the line of scrimmage; their first priority is to stop the opponent's passing game.

smash mouth A style of offense that relies on the running game.

FURTHER READING

BOOKS

Saban, Nick, and Brian Curtis. *How Good Do You Want to Be?* New York, NY: Ballantine Books, 2005.

Yaeger, Don. *Great Teams: 16 Things High Performing Organizations Do Differently*. Nashville, TN: Thomas Nelson, 2016.

WEBSITES

Alabama Crimson Tide Football

http://www.rolltide.com/index.aspx?path=football

Get an inside look at the Crimson Tide, with interviews, news, stats, game previews, and more.

The Nick's Kids Foundation

http://www.nickskidsfoundation.org

Nonprofit organization dedicated to raising awareness and resources for deserving organizations throughout the state of Alabama and the Southeast.

FILMS

The Blind Side. Alcon Entertainment, 2009.

Nick Saban: Gamechanger. Flashlight Media Group, 2010.

Roll Tide/War Eagle. ESPN, 2011.